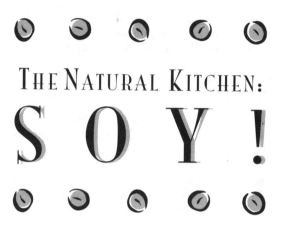

THE NATURAL KITCHEN:
S O Y !

75 Delicious Ways to

Enjoy Nature's Miracle Food

DANA JACOBI

PRIMA PUBLISHING

PRIMA PUBLISHING and colophon are registered trademarks of Prima Communications, Inc.

The author wishes to acknowledge *Natural Health* magazine. Some of the information and recipes in this book appeared in other versions in that magazine.

The table "Varieties of Miso" on pages 12–13 is adapted from *The Book of Miso,* © 1983 by William Shurtleff and Akiko Aoyagi, with permission of Ten Speed Press.

Library of Congress Cataloging-in-Publication Data

Jacobi, Dana.
    The natural kitchen : soy! : 75 delicious ways to enjoy nature's miracle food / Dana Jacobi.
        p.   cm.   (Natural kitchen)
    Includes bibliographical references and index.
    ISBN 0-7615-0478-8
    1. Cookery (Soybeans) 2. Soyfoods. I. Title. II. Series.
TX803.S6J33   1996
641.6′ 5655—dc20   96-27634
                                                         CIP

    97 98 99 00 01 AA 10 9 8 7 6 5 4 3 2
Printed in the United States of America

How to Order
Single copies may be ordered from Prima Publishing, P.O. Box 1260BK, Rocklin, CA 95677; telephone (916) 632-4400. Quantity discounts are also available. On your letterhead, include information concerning the intended use of the books and the number of books you wish to purchase.

Visit us online at http://www.primapublishing.com

CONTENTS

PREFACE

THIS IS A COOKBOOK THAT I PASSIONately wanted to write. Its inspiration was my desire to share new ways of cooking with soyfoods that show off their versatility and adaptability. While this book includes some information on the health benefits of soyfoods and the meatless diet they so richly support, it mainly introduces you to soyfoods and pleasing ways to make them a part of your daily diet.

If you are new to soy, you will find descriptions of soyfoods, from tofu and soymilk to less familiar soy ingredients like miso, tempeh, and textured vegetable protein (TVP), all of which can be found in most natural food stores or ethnic groceries.

If you already cook with soyfoods, the approximately 75 recipes in this book and their variations will expand your repertoire. These recipes will take you across lines that people who cook with soy rarely approach. The dishes bring familiar and satisfying textures along with flavors that are full and deep. Whether ethnic or classic, they are dishes with verve and elegance. They express my own way of eating, which along with soy, spinach, broccoli, carrots, strawberries, grains, and all the other good stuff includes plenty of chocolate and indulgent desserts. For a good life, I think we should eat and enjoy them all.

ACKNOWLEDGMENTS

THANKS TO MY PARENTS, WITH WHOM I first tasted tofu at The Great Shanghai on 125th Street. Next, my gratitude goes to Bill Shurtleff, whose writings electrified me into wanting to taste and learn more about the entire world of soyfoods—you have been a fountain of information and a stickler for detail. Thanks to Mark Messina, whose work galvanized me to create food for people who understand the importance of eating soy and want to eat well.

In conceiving and producing this work, thanks go to Mark Bittman; little did I realize that your assignments would be the catalyst for this book. Also to Jennifer Basye Sander, my editor at Prima, who saw the opportunity for soy; to my agent, Martha Casselman, who encouraged me through the writing with infinite patience; and to Irena Chalmers, who helped give this work its name. At Prima, thanks to Dan Foster for shepherding the work into print with such care.

In developing and testing the recipes, my appreciation goes to Ronnie Matalan, and to the intrepid soy tasters: Amelia Adams, Sara Amelar, Fern Berman, Adelaide Camillo, Dalia Carmel, Cara De Silva, Ellen Greaves, David Karp, Dr. Jacqueline Newman, Rosa Lo San Ross, and Li Wong Shang.

It would be impossible to thank individually each of the soyfoods artisans and manufacturers who answered my endless questions, but special appreciation to the Elwells and the folks at Wildwood.

Eternal thanks to Joan Emery for her support, confidence, and coaching. Also to Barney Stein and Susan Dereczky for their expert eyes. Blessings to Nadine Ellman for support at essential moments. Last, but not least, bless you, Iris Carullo: Without your help, this work might still be somewhere in my computer.

INTRODUCTION

THOUGH I FIRST TASTED TOFU IN 1953, at the precocious age of eight, my serious intrigue with soy began in 1978 when I read *The Book of Tofu* and *The Book of Miso,* both by William Shurtleff and Akiko Aoyagi. This fascination increased during the early 1980s as I discovered dishes made with soyfoods at the growing number of still-obscure Asian restaurants in New York and anywhere else I traveled to around the U.S. and in Europe. I also sought out natural food restaurants in order to sample every kind of soyfood and to experience ways of using them. Any soy item I found in health food stores, I bought.

Many of the foods I found were so appealing that I wanted to share them. Beyond friends, though, few people were receptive to trying these unfamiliar foods. Eager to spread my soy enthusiasm, I embarked on a benign deception. Proving that anyone I dined with or cooked for could enjoy soy became a game. Since I was already in the food business and it was the food-crazed '80s, there were lots of opportunities to play. Most of all, in the catering service I operated, I loved to sneak soy onto the menu. The posher the party, the more likely I was to include a bean curd-based dip or miso-sparked gravy. If an investment banker or Park Avenue client requested a vegetarian main course, I would often modify a chicken or meat dish, replacing the animal ingredient with tofu or tempeh.

As concerns about cholesterol, saturated fat, and reducing the consumption of animal foods grew into a national obsession, opportunities to present soy cooking to a wider audience opened up. Then, to further expand interest in eating soy, the media was filled with news about health benefits to be gained from eating soyfoods, ranging from lowering blood cholesterol levels, fighting cancer, and relieving symptoms of menopause, to possibly helping to reduce the risk of breast cancer. Finally, what clinched my own commitment to soyfoods was finding out that I was post-menopausal. As I said, this is a cookbook, not a health book. But finding myself on the far side of a voyage that turned out to be a non-event—not one hot flash or episode of emotions run amok, just brief, occasional periods of restless sleep and flagging of energy—I realized that the soy I had been eating might have eased my way through an important passage.

Soy and Health

When results of the study by Dr. James W. Anderson of the Veterans Affairs Medical Center in Lexington, Kentucky, hit the press in 1995, the growing interest in soyfoods accelerated to warp speed. In his synthesis of results from 29 scientific reports covering 700 subjects, Anderson found that including 47 grams of soy protein per day cut serum cholesterol levels by an average of 9.3 percent in just one month. Since a 10 to 15 percent reduction results in a 20 to 30 percent reduction in the risk of coronary heart disease, this is a significant finding.

These data are in addition to material emerging from study of a host of phytochemicals (biologically active substances found only in plants). Some of these phytochemicals are found only in soybeans. They appear to be potent cancer inhibitors, particularly genistein and other isoflavones, phytates, saponins, and protease inhibitors. In their book, *The Simple Soybean and Your Health* (Avery Publishing, 1995), Mark Messina, Ph.D., and Virginia Messina explain that these anticarcinogens work in various ways, adding that "some directly prevent tumors from developing." Others evidently slow or halt the growth of existing tumors.

For women, soyfoods appear to offer important protection against breast cancer, thanks to their abundance of phytoestrogens like isoflavones, including genistein. Mark Messina explains that these are considered weak forms of estrogen. As such, he elaborates, they work by occupying the same receptors on breast cells to which the hormone estrogen normally affixes. While apparently doing some of the same work as estrogen, the milder phytoestrogens seem not to trigger some of its cancer-enhancing effects. Soy's phytochemicals also appear to have benefits in relation to prostate cancer in men.

To date, many health claims for soy are based on anecdotal evidence rather than scientifically controlled studies. A number of studies are underway to substantiate further claims, such as the one being conducted by Dr. Susan Potter at the University of Illinois with postmenopausal women subjects, looking at the effects of soy on cholesterol levels and other conditions.

Growing awareness of the benefits of eating a plant-based diet is also stimulating interest in soy. As people cut back on animal foods, they are unsure of how to obtain certain nutrients in their diet. Meeting protein needs is a particular concern. Protein-rich soyfoods are seen as a simple way to meet this requirement. Nutritionally, soybeans offer the highest-quality protein of any plant food, containing all eight essential amino acids. They are a good source of omega-3 fatty acids. Certain soyfoods, including tempeh and *okara*, are also a good source of fiber—an element often lacking in the American diet.

Despite the favorable indications, I don't declare soyfoods to be magic. For example, in menopause, many factors contribute to one's experience. Still, in my case, negative factors were stacked against me, and yet the process was barely noticeable. This convinced me that soy should be as much a part of our everyday diet as fruits and vegetables.

How will you accomplish this if you have had little experience with soyfoods beyond bean curd, mostly dumped into stir-fries or marinated in soy sauce and grilled? Or if you have tried soy-burgers and soymilk and didn't like them? My own experience may be useful here, too.

To be content, I have to be well fed. That means eating food that is sensually gratifying, as well as sensible and natural. Pleasure from food means more to me than banishing every last gram of fat or measure of refined sweetness from a recipe. To provide dishes with pleasure as well as the goodness of soy, while working on the recipes in this book I concentrated on creating beautiful, exciting food with vivid flavors and satisfying textures. This is also natural cooking, prepared from mostly fresh and minimally processed ingredients. In some dishes, the soy turns out to be the most highly processed ingredient—a choice I made when a particular soyfood would be the most appealing form and would provide healthful benefits.

Cooking exquisite natural food is easier now than ever, because the quality of organic and natural foods has improved so much during the past decade. Visit any of the natural food stores blossoming all over the country, from supermarkets like Whole Foods and Wild Oats to independents like The Mustard Seed in Akron, Ohio, and you'll see how health food has transformed into appealing and even outstanding food. You'll find chocolate bars as divine as Godiva, organic dairy products so fresh and good that the best chefs prefer them, and minimally refined sweeteners suited to making desserts that taste as good as they look. Organic produce today is usually jewel-perfect and full of flavor as nature meant it.

This book shows how to combine natural ingredients in dishes that break new ground in the definition of good food. This is my idea of working magic with soy.

ALL ABOUT
SOYFOODS

There are many ways to add soy to your diet and to increase the amount of soy you eat. You can cook from scratch, using traditional soyfoods like tofu (also known as bean curd), tempeh, and miso in Asian recipes or in all kinds of salads, soups, stews, dips, and other dishes. You can use lightly transformed soyfoods like smoked tofu and marinated tempeh. When there's no time to cook, you can buy fresh, prepared foods made with a host of different soyfoods.

Beyond the traditional soyfoods, there is another level of soy choices. These are more highly processed foods designed to resemble other foods we are used to. They include prepared tofu burgers and soymilk. Then there is an ever-growing list of soy-based "replacers" and convenience foods. These refined products include everything from meat-imitating soy burgers and hot dogs to creamy frozen desserts, soy cheeses, pizza topped with soy cheese, and frozen lasagna.

The supermarket where you shop probably carries tofu and soymilk. Ninety-five percent of U.S. supermarkets do, according to Bill Shurtleff, who heads the Soyfoods Center in Lafayette, California, and who has written several definitive books about soy. Maybe the influence of emigration from China, Japan, Vietnam, and Korea into communities all over the country has touched you, raising your awareness of traditional soyfoods beyond bean curd to tempeh and miso. Or you may be eyeing the growing number of Americanized soyfoods appearing both in supermarkets and on restaurant menus, from lasagna and burgers to cheesecake and frozen desserts.

Following is an explanation of all the kinds of soyfood available, either as ingredients or in ready-to-eat foods. It shows the astonishing range of soy possibilities—in flavor, texture, and versatility—and recipes demonstrating how to use them.

TRADITIONAL SOYFOODS

Soybeans have been a principle source of protein in eastern Asia for at least 2,000 years. Many Asians eat some form of soy every day. To make the protein in soybeans more easily available, as well as to add variety to their daily diet, Asians have transformed soybeans in many ways, using methods that evolved over centuries in villages and on farms. In the West, tofu, soy sauce, and, to a lesser degree, miso and tempeh are the best known soy products from Asia. The methods for making these foods remain simple even when they are commercially produced in large quantity. That is why tofu, miso, tempeh, and soy sauce are often categorized as traditional soyfoods.

Tofu

Surprisingly, it was Benjamin Franklin who brought tofu to America in the late 1770s after discovering it in France. It remained unknown to most people despite the flood of Chinese immigrants flowing into the United States to work on the railroads during the 1800s. Their demand for familiar ingredients to use in their cooking led to the establishment of the first commercial tofu shop, Quong Hop, in San Francisco in 1906. The company is still in business, providing tofu to both the Asian community and to natural food stores in Northern California, under the name Soy Deli.

Some adventurous Americans discovered bean curd dishes in Chinese restaurants during the 1950s. But most of us associate tofu with the counterculture of the late 1960s and 1970s, when *The Book of Tofu* by William Shurtleff and Akiko Aoyagi appeared to serve as both a Book of Revelations and the Bible for tofu. Since then, concerns about cholesterol, saturated fat, lactose-intolerance, and unwelcome substances in animal foods, as well as ethical reasons for following a meatless diet, have pushed tofu into the supermarket if not into the mainstream American diet.

Tofu is cholesterol-free, a great source of protein, and high in calcium, as you will see shortly. Ethically and ecologically, it is a friendly food. The sensory qualities Asians prize in tofu—its custard-soft texture, subtle flavor, and generally low-key personality—turn off those Americans who describe it as mushy, bland, and boring. For them, there are brilliant ways to transform tofu.

To make tofu, dried soybeans are soaked overnight and ground up, then cooked and pressed to separate the soy milk from the fibers of the soybean. The pulpy, fibrous mass left after the liquid has been extracted is called *okara*. In Asia, it is also used as a food.

The next steps depend on whether the bean curd to be produced is the firm ivory blocks and pillows most of us know simply as tofu, and which the Japanese call "cotton" tofu, or if the end result is to be silken tofu, a more custard-like form of bean curd whose popularity in the U.S. is growing rapidly. To make regular bean curd, the process of coagulating soymilk and processing the curd resembles cheese-making, with the soy curds separated from the whey. For silken tofu, the steps are closer to those for making yogurt, in which milk is coagulated but there is no separation of curds and whey.

For regular tofu, the soymilk is coagulated in huge, steam-jacketed kettles. As they form, the curds are turned. The tofu-maker's trick lies in knowing just when to break up the curds. The bean curd will be grainy if this is done too soon.

Calcium sulfate, a naturally mined substance also known as gypsum, and Epsom salts, or calcium chloride, are the coagulants most frequently used in tofu-making. Along with forming a curd, they increase the calcium content in tofu. *Nigari*, a natural form of magnesium chloride extracted from sea water, was the first coagulant used. It is still favored by some tofu-makers because it can make a sweeter-tasting product.

When the curd for regular tofu has cooked for about an hour and reached just the right point, it is turned into cheesecloth-lined stainless steel cheese boxes and weighted. This pressing removes the whey. The amount of liquid drained off determines whether the finished product will be soft, firm, or extra firm. Finally, tofu is cooled as quickly as possible from 150 degrees down to 35 degrees in a refrigerated tank filled with cold water. It is then cut, weighed, and sealed in tubs or pouches for sale.

The soymilk used in making silken tofu is thicker. Lactone, a natural product made from cornstarch, is used along with the calcium chloride. After the soymilk coagulates, it is drained and pressed. Or, in a process even closer to making yogurt, the soymilk with coagulant is poured directly into the tub or aseptic box in which it will be sold. Like regular tofu, silken bean curd comes in textures from soft to solidly firm. Whether quiveringly delicate or Jell-O dense, this tofu shatters easily and purees beautifully.

Taste If you have used more than one brand of tofu, you have probably noticed that they differ widely in flavor and texture. One of the most useful things I did in getting to know tofu was to conduct a tasting. It included ten examples of silken tofu, in textures from soft to extra firm, and 20 examples of regular tofu in the same range of textures. Some of the brands were local or regional (to either the East or the West Coast) and some national. A few examples came from tofu shops in New York City's Chinatown.

I think the twelve people who joined me in this tasting were even more struck than I was by the variety of flavors and textures. Some of the bean curd was nutty and mild; some tasted flat, earthy, or "beany." A few brands tasted sour or even burnt. Proving just how much two simple ingredients—soybeans and water—can produce different results, we found that examples made by Nasoya, Azumaya, and Vitasoy, all brands from the same company, were profoundly different in taste.

What produces such variation? Everything from the variety of soybeans used and the water to the cooking process and the time elapsed since the tofu was made. Knowing all this, you can appreciate the skill of large manufacturers, including White Wave, Mori-Nu, Soy Deli, Kikkoman, and Vitasoy, in maintaining fairly consistent flavor. Personally, when the flavor of tofu will not be heavily covered by other ingredients in a dish, I favor the clean, pleasantly nutty flavor of the regular bean curd made by Wildwood Natural Foods. Their bean curd is made from Clear Hilum soybeans grown for them in Minnesota. When silken tofu is called for, I use Nasoya or Mori-Nu silken tofu because the Kikkoman I have bought always seems to taste very beany.

Since taste is a personal matter, I urge you to select two or three brands of bean curd at the stores where you shop most often, buying a couple of textures from each one, and set up a little tasting. This will let you find the ones that best suit you. You will find many brands of regular tofu made from organic soybeans. Organic silken tofu is much less common.

Texture Texture is another aspect of the tofu-maker's art. Whether it is soft, firm, or extra firm, you'll see variations from creamy and smooth to spongy, rubbery, or grainy. Beyond aesthetic differences in texture—graininess is never pleasant—density is important when cooking with tofu. Even with delicate silken tofu, whether soft textured or firm, you'll find differences from brand to brand.

Firm and extra firm tofu appeal most to people because they are chewy. They also hold together best during cooking. Mainly, they are cut into cubes for stir-frying or into slabs for marinating and grilling or baking.

Silken tofu purees beautifully because of its high water content. It is an ideal base for dressings, dips, and toppings. It also has an elegant quality when cut into cubes and served in light soups. Avoid silken tofu in stir-fries, stews, and such. Even the extra firm kind tends to break up when stirred or cooked for a length of time.

Unfortunately, picking tofu by texture can get a bit dicey. Using soft or firm silken tofu or a soft regular tofu may produce virtually the same result in some recipes when the bean curd is pureed. This variability—bothersome when you don't know what to expect—can actually be a boon if your local store does not carry exactly what a recipe calls for.

The same variability exists at the more compacted range of bean curd. Here too, density is not the same with every brand. Gourmet Firm Nigari Tofu from Soy Deli is the densest of them all; it's a tofu I can almost always use without pressing.

As with taste, finding the right texture is a matter of trying what your market carries. Do this just once, and you'll see which tofu has the combination of texture and flavor that pleases you the most.

The Nutritional Value of Tofu Tofu is one of the few vegan foods to offer complete protein. Its protein is also in a highly available form; the body should be able to use it as well as it uses chicken and almost as well as it uses beef. Yet bean curd contains significantly fewer calories per gram than these animal proteins.

Providing the nutritive content of bean curd in one set of numbers is about as easy as grabbing a fistful of silken tofu. The problem: Recommended serving size varies from 3 ounces to 5¼ ounces, while fat, protein, and calories per serving also vary by type of tofu and by brand. Hence, a 3½-ounce serving of firm tofu made by one company may have 90 calories, 11 grams protein, and get 45 percent of its calories from fat, while the same size serving of another brand has 70 calories, 8 grams of protein, and 50 percent of its calories from fat.

The firmer the bean curd, the lower the water content and the denser the nutrient content. Denser tofu also has relatively more fat per serving. If the fat content of tofu concerns you, remember you are getting good-quality nutrients, with no cholesterol, minimal saturated fat, and important phytochemicals. Also, the percentage of fat in your finished dish is lowered by the addition of other ingredients.

If you strongly wish to minimize your consumption of fat, use reduced-fat firm regular tofu. It contains about one-third fewer grams of fat per serving. The process for removing fat in regular tofu is mechanical. When the beans are hulled and flaked, a portion of their oil is removed. This bean curd is fine in most recipes calling for regular tofu. With silken tofu, you also have choices, although Mori-Nu's regular or full-fat firm silken tofu has only 2.5 grams of fat per 3-ounce serving. They also make fat-free extra firm tofu and the same texture with 1 percent fat, or 1 gram per 3-ounce serving.

Miso

My introduction to miso was probably the same as yours—in miso soup at a Japanese restaurant. Perhaps you have noticed that this soup varies in color from a creamy ivory beige to the rich brown of beef bouillon. It may taste noticeably sweet or dark and salty. This is because the miso used in making this soup comes in a seemingly infinite range of tastes, from sweet and mild to salty, earthy, even meaty; of tones from pale golden beige to terra cotta and espresso black; and of textures from smooth as peanut butter to chunky as baked beans. Miso, also called fermented bean paste, has a unique ability to add complex flavor and to enrich the texture of all kinds of dishes.

This cultured, fermented food is usually made from a combination of soybeans and rice, though barley or more soybeans may also be used in place of the grain. Names like mellow barley, hatcho, and genmai are only vaguely descriptive of types of miso. Even names that seem specific don't mean what you might think. For example, both brown rice and mugi (barley) miso contain soybeans. People allergic to soy can try chickpea miso, the only kind made without soy.

The complex flavors and distinctive texture of natural miso develop through the process of fermentation and aging, which may be allowed to go on for up to three years. To make miso, a grain or a part of the soybeans is inoculated with *Aspergillus orzyae* bacteria; this cooked, cultured medium is called *koji*. The rest of the soybeans and grain are cooked and washed, then combined with the *koji* and salt. This mixture is set to ferment. During fermentation, the lactobacillus, yeasts, and other microorganisms and enzymes from the bacteria convert the sugars in the beans and rice or other grain to carbohydrates, break the proteins down into amino acids, and the fat into fatty acids.

In traditionally made miso, fermentation is active only during the heat of summer. During the winter, the cold stops the fermentation. This "rest" helps to kill off nonbeneficial bacteria and enzymes. Most commercially made, or "quick," miso is usually pushed to contract the fermentation process into a few days or weeks by using a heated environment. Then, bleach, sweetener, or other additives may be used to simulate the look and taste of natural miso.

Artisanal miso-makers like Christian and Margaret Elwell of South River Farm in Conway, Massachusetts, say the number of summers a miso goes through before it is packaged determines its age. According to William Shurtleff and Akiko Aoyagi in *The Book of Miso* (Ten Speed Press, 1983), the more usual way of dating miso is by the number of calendar years it has seen. For example, miso started in the fall and harvested a year later is called "two-year" miso, although it is actually only 12 months old. Likewise, "three-year" misos are often only 18 months old. This method of dating ties in with the common Asian practice of adding a year of age to people at each New Year.

The Origins of Miso   The precursor of miso was a fermented mixture known as *chiang*. It originated in China 2,500 years ago. Buddhist monks brought it to Japan in the seventh century, where it evolved into the miso we know today. This fermented food also traveled to Korea, where it is called *jang*. In some form or other, various kinds of *chiang* are used in cooking throughout East and Southeast Asia. Nowhere, though, has fermented bean paste become as much a staple as in Japan, where perhaps 70 percent of the population starts the day with a bowl of steaming miso soup. Japanese consumption of miso typically equals several tablespoons per day.

For Americans, awareness of miso began in the early '60s, mainly through the counterculture and macrobiotics. Even with the growing number of Japanese restaurants, sushi shops, and Japanese food stores, and the availability of miso in virtually every natural food store, it remains little known compared to tofu. Chefs playing with Asian flavors are fast catching on to it, though, so awareness of miso is increasing.

In *The Book of Miso,* William Shurtleff takes 11 pages to describe the full panoply of misos. I've adapted the following chart from his book, outlining the three major miso families, two special groups, and more than 29 varieties.

The best way to understand the personality of different misos and see how you might use them in cooking is to sample them. A formal tasting is a great way to find the misos you like. Organize your tasting just as you might if you were sampling wine, lining up a group of friends and buying as many kinds of miso as you can find in local stores or obtain by mail order. (Since miso costs $5 to $8 a pound, a group tasting also lets you spread the cost.)

Varieties of Miso

Group	Type	Variety	Flavor	Color	Natural Aging Time	Some Japanese Names and Subvarieties	Protein %	Carbohydrate %	Salt %
REGULAR MISO	Rice Miso	Red Miso (includes Brown Rice Miso)	Deep, rich saltiness	Reddish brown to russet	6 to 12 months	Aka Miso, Genmai Miso, Sendai Miso	13.5	19.1	13.0
		Light-Yellow Miso	Mature rounded saltiness with subtle tartness	Bright light yellow	1 to 2 years	Shinshu Miso, Akita Miso	13.5	19.6	12.5
		Mellow Red Miso	Deep semisweetness	Yellowish red	3 to 6 months	Aka Miso	11.2	27.9	13.0
		Mellow Beige Miso	Light semisweetness	Yellow to tan	5 to 20 days	Tanshoku Miso, Mochigomé Miso	13.0	29.1	7.0
		Mellow White Miso	Rich, heady mellowness	Light beige	4 weeks	Shiro-koji Miso	12.3	27.5	9.1
		Sweet Red Miso	Rich, deep sweetness	Lustrous reddish brown	10 to 30 days	Edo Ama-miso	12.7	31.7	6.0
		Sweet White Miso	Light, rich dessert-like sweetness	Ivory to yellowish white	1 to 4 weeks	Shiro Miso, Saikyo Miso, Sanuki Miso	11.1	35.9	5.5

Barley Miso	Barley Miso	Deep, rich saltiness	Dark reddish brown	1 to 3 years	Mugi Miso	12.8	21.0	13.0
	Mellow Barley Miso	Deep, rich subtle sweetness	Yellowish brown to russet	10 to 20 days	Mugi Miso	11.1	29.8	10.0
Soybean Miso	Hatcho Miso	Mellow richness, subtly tart	Chocolate brown	18 to 36 months	Hatcho Miso	21.0	12.0	10.6
	Soybean Miso	Mellow saltiness	Dark reddish brown	1 year	Mamé Miso	19.4	13.2	11.2
SPECIAL MISO Finger Lickin' Miso	Namémiso Natto	Rich, fermented sweetness	Golden brown to dark amber	20 to 60 days	Namémiso	11.0	30.0	8.0
MODERN MISO Modern Miso	Akadashi Miso	Rich, mellow sweetness	Dark reddish brown	1 to 12 months	Akadashi Miso	16.0	31.9	10.0
	Chickpea Miso	Mellow, subtle chickpea flavor	Beige	1 to 3 months		1.0		7.0

Adapted from *The Book of Miso* by William Shurtleff and Akiko Aoyagi.

At the end, there will probably be enough left for everyone to take home some of their favorite ones.

While getting to know miso, I set up a tasting with 38 misos. There were American brands and Japanese-made miso packaged for U.S. companies. Among the things I learned: The best way to taste miso is on the tip of a chopstick. And the best way to clear your palate during a tasting is by sipping plain hot water.

In the tasting, five misos came out as particular favorites. The most popular was chickpea miso from Miso Master in Rutherford, North Carolina. John Belleme, an American trained in Japan by the last of a centuries-old line of miso-makers, says Rutherford is the place in America with the ideal climate for making miso. The next most-liked spots are (in order) South River's dark, rich barley miso; Westbrae's three-year-old hatcho miso, with its chocolatey undertones; and Westbrae's aka miso, with its good balance between salt and other flavors. Natto miso, a sweetly zesty, relish-like blend containing whole barley, slivers of ginger, and *kombu* (a sea vegetable) also got a lot of votes; this miso, made by Ohsawa in Japan and distributed by Gold Mine Natural Food Company in San Diego, California, is sold in bulk at natural food stores and in plastic tubs. For a special experience, I like South River's deep, dark, chunky dandelion-leek miso. This blend of black soybeans, brown rice, and miso-pickled wild leek, dandelion, and Maine coast kelp offers such exquisitely full, clear flavor that it should be enjoyed only in a simple miso soup. It has a presence as complex as Romanée Conti, the *ne plus ultra* of wines.

Miso, Nutrition, and Health   On average, miso contains 12 to 13 percent protein by weight, with hatcho miso providing a substantial 20 percent. This is comparable to the level of protein in chicken (20 percent) and eggs (13 percent). It provides complementary proteins because it is made from beans and grain; this means up to 72 percent of the protein in miso is available to the body. The complementary pairing of beans and grain in miso also means that using it makes the protein in the dish you are preparing more available to the body.

Miso's Enzymes and Digestion   As a fermented food, miso contains enzymes, which increase the body's ability to use the nutrients in both the miso and in the foods with which it's eaten. The wealth of natural enzymes produced by the lactobacillus, yeasts, and other microorganisms in unpasteurized miso stimulate digestion. Some misos contain live cultures, while others are pasteurized, which means they no longer are living foods. Look for unpasteurized miso packaged in round plastic tubs in the refrigerator case at natural and Japanese food stores.

Miso sold in plastic bags is generally pasteurized. This process makes it possible to seal the miso in plastic bags without risk of the bags swelling or exploding because of carbon dioxide gas given off by living bioorganisms. Read miso labels to verify what you are getting, even though you may have to take what you see with a grain of salt. For example, Eden Foods does not mention pasteurization on their bags, but the company told me that the product is pasteurized. Hatcho miso is the one variety that, because of its high salt content, generates so little carbon dioxide that it can be bagged without pasteurization.

Miso Promotes Resistance to Disease   Proponents of a macrobiotic diet say miso promotes resistance to disease by alkalizing the body. Scientists seem to be finding that soyfoods, including miso, do boost the immune system. Some reports also claim that miso cleanses the body of toxins, from nicotine to radiation.

Sodium Content   The salt in miso acts as a natural preservative. It slows down the fermentation process, providing proper time for yeasts and bacteria in the *koji* and any "seed miso" mixed in from a previous batch to do their work. Some people view the salt in miso as a reason to avoid using it. Miso contains only 8 to 14 percent salt, with much of its intense and complex flavor coming from the action of fermentation on the other ingredients it contains. Since salt is 40 percent sodium, this means ½ ounce of miso—about a tablespoon—containing 12 percent salt provides 680 milligrams of sodium, while 1 tablespoon of straight salt gives you 6,589 milligrams of sodium; and the salt does not include any of the lecithin, linoleic acid, and B_{12} that are hard to get in a vegan diet, as well as other beneficial substances.

People with high blood pressure or sensitivity to sodium should avoid miso. Others may view cooking with miso in a new light. The salt content in miso actually is modest enough that cooking with it does not eliminate the need for salt in a dish. It enhances the taste but does not give that "lift" in flavor only salt can provide.

Miso Is Like Wine Traditionally from opposite sides of the globe, miso and wine have much in common. Both are fermented and living foods whose flavors take shape and alter over time. Both are influenced by conditions of place: Just like wine, a miso made in one village has a decidedly different taste, and even texture, from another one made using identical ingredients in a village only miles away.

Today, most miso is industrially made in huge batches, using heat to accelerate the fermentation process, chemical additives to adjust its flavor, color, and texture, and preservatives to do what nature has not had time to complete. But, like the best wines, good-quality miso is a natural, traditionally-made product crafted by artisans. Fine miso is identified by vintage, just like good wine. Perhaps even more unexpectedly, as with wine, the traditional method involves treading the soybeans underfoot to crush them. The blended mash of beans, salt, and *koji* is then aged in huge wooden vats made of cedar or cypress. Ultimately, in both miso and wine, color and aroma only hint at the mouth-filling wonders in their taste.

Tempeh

Tempeh, a staple in Indonesia, consists of cooked soybeans bound together by whitish threads, called *mycelium,* to form thin slabs. I have eaten tempeh in earnestly prepared but flat-tasting dishes in health food restaurants and in exquisitely spiced dishes in Indonesian restaurants. When it is well prepared, many people find this the most meaty of the traditional soyfoods. They like it for its texture and for the taste, which ranges from mild and beany to a full mushroomy and even yeasty flavor.

As an ingredient, this is a remarkably versatile soyfood. In squares or cubes, you can marinate and grill tempeh for burgers and kebabs. It's good diced and braised in stews, chopped and incorporated into sauces, or ground to use as a base for pâtés and spreads. In a felicitous marriage of East and West, one of my favorite tempeh dishes is, in effect, a curried Waldorf salad, which has cubes of tempeh braised in apple juice and curry powder added to the usual diced apple, celery, onions, and chopped walnuts. Fortunately, a natural food store in New York City called Natural Frontier sells this salad at their deli counter, so I don't have to make it.

Today, tempeh-making is still the simple process it was when it began in Java, where its production has been documented since the early 1800s. This process starts with lightly cooking and hulling split soybeans, then inoculating them with *Rhizopus oligosporus* bacteria. The beans are then formed into inch-thick cakes on trays, which are stacked and set in a warm, moist place and left to ferment for about 24 hours. When the tempeh reaches the desired state, bound together by the *mycelium* (the white threads of a friendly mold), the supple yet firm slabs are cut into rectangles. They are now ready to use.

Modern, industrialized tempeh-making remains remarkably similar to what is still done in the thousands of little tempeh shops. The difference is that the inoculated beans are sealed in individual plastic bags sized to hold a finished cake of tempeh, usually weighing 8 ounces. The bags are perforated with tiny holes so gasses and heat generated during fermentation can escape. The bags are laid out in one layer on trays, which are stacked in a sanitary, heat-controlled chamber to incubate. When a nice, velvety, grayish-white matrix of mycelium has developed, the tempeh is shrink-wrapped, vacuum-packed, and blanched or frozen to help retard further fermentation. Tempeh is sold from the refrigerated dairy or deli case.

During fermentation, transformations take place that make tempeh a particularly rich and usable source of nutrients. Enzymes from the bacteria digest some of the nutrients in the beans, making their protein more available. Along with the cooking, the fermentation process greatly reduces the oligosaccharides, which are natural sugars in the beans; for many people, these are the culprits that cause flatulence. As a result, people who have problems with soymilk or products containing TVP may well enjoy eating tempeh.

Tempeh is often made from a combination of soybeans and one or more grains or some other filler. While all-soy tempeh has a pronounced flavor with a faintly bitter aftertaste, the blended tempeh is milder tasting. In Asia, wheat, peanuts, or *okara* are likely fillers. In the U.S., rice, millet, quinoa, or barley are most often used. American manufacturers also add sesame seeds, sea vegetables, or dehydrated vegetables to flavor tempeh.

Western culture discovered tempeh through the Dutch colonization of Indonesia. During World War II, many prisoners of war held in Indonesian prison camps owed their lives to the tempeh they ate.

In 1962, Asians opened the first tempeh shop (as a tempeh production facility is properly called) for producing this soyfood in the U.S. In 1975, the first tempeh shop run by non-Asians was set up in Onadilla, Nebraska, and The Farm, a commune in Summertown, Tennessee, offered recipes using tempeh in their popular *Farm Vegetarian Cookbook*. Additional articles that appeared in *Organic Gardening* and *Prevention* magazines also promoted tempeh. This activity established tempeh as a protein choice for a devoted, if small, group of Americans.

If more people understood tempeh, I think they would use it. Fortunately, along with the increasing availability of plain tempeh to use as an ingredient, there are also lots of tempeh burgers all ready to throw on the grill. Some are bathed in zesty marinades with flavors ranging from lemon or garlic and herbs to classic barbecue. And there's Fakin' Bacon, a unique and useful ingredient for putting smoky flavor into meatless dishes.

Usually, tempeh is steamed or fried before it is added to a dish. Steaming makes the tempeh taste milder and gives it a softer texture. Frying tempeh, or just browning it in a pan sprayed with nonstick cooking spray, adds appealing color and crispness that remain even after it has been immersed in a stew or soup. Tempeh also marinates beautifully.

A Nutritional Note   Some health food literature lists tempeh as a source of vitamin B_{12}. When vitamin B_{12} appears, it is the result of benign contamination with bacteria not normally part of the tempeh-making process. Because of the sanitary conditions prevailing in this country, American-made tempeh is not likely to contain this vitamin.

Soy Sauce

A whole book could be devoted to the history and manufacturing of this flavorful condiment. In Japan alone, the government recognizes five kinds of shoyu (naturally fermented soy sauce) made with wheat and cooked soybeans. Then there is the question of tamari—which is variously defined as the liquid wept by miso as it ferments, as a soy sauce made without wheat, and as a form of naturally brewed soy sauce. Soy sauce is not rich in the phytochemicals attracting positive attention to soyfoods. Also, it is an ingredient familiar to most Americans. So, while it would be interesting to talk about fine-quality Asian and domestically made natural soy sauces, that will have to wait for another time.

Soymilk

Liquid soymilk is made from cooked, ground soybeans. It is good for everything from pouring on cereal and making smoothies to cooking. Maybe that is why it is one of the fastest-selling natural food products found in most conventional supermarkets in the U.S. as well as all natural food stores. Dry or powdered soymilk is another matter, as you will see later.

You may notice that the word "soymilk" never appears on this product, because according to the USDA Standards of Identity, only "lactational secretion from mammals" can be called milk. Packages instead use the terms "beverage" or "drink." But cooks and others, finding soy "beverage" too cumbersome and vague, often use the term "soymilk," as you see it here.

Soymilk, like other major soyfoods, originated in Asia. Most Asian markets in the U.S. sell it, fresh, in the refrigerator case, but the thin texture and beany taste of this milk, simply made from soybeans and water, is palatable to few people not raised on it.

To accommodate American preferences, brands sold in supermarkets and natural food stores are produced less like the traditional soyfood made for Asians and more like a high-tech product. They usually contain flavoring—vanilla, chocolate, or carob and a natural sweetener like barley malt. They also may contain oil and a thickening agent such as carrageenan or job's tears (a kind of barley). These ingredients give the liquid a feel like cow's milk in the mouth. You will find soymilk that has fat removed—choose from 2 percent fat, 1 percent fat, or fat-free—and calcium-fortified soymilk.

Most of the soymilk offered in supermarkets and food stores comes in aseptic, shelf-stable 1-liter packs or in single-serve boxes like fruit juice. Soymilk in this packaging is good for a year before opening. Fresh soymilk, sold in bottles from the refrigerator case, is also available in some stores. White Wave, exploring whether soymilk has a broader appeal when presented exactly like cow's milk, is now offering a product called "Silk" in familiar-looking quart and half-gallon gable-topped milk cartons.

Different manufacturers offer some or all of the following: regular (with full-fat and no flavoring but some sweetener), calcium-fortified, flavored, full-fat, low-fat, fat-free, and unsweetened soymilk. In the "Cooking with Soyfoods" section later, I will explain how these differ in texture and flavor and how these differences affect cooking with them. I suggest tasting a variety of brands and different types to see what you like best for drinking, on cereal, and in coffee.

Powdered soymilk is not made from milk extracted from the bean and dehydrated, but from finely ground soybean flour. It lasts a long time on the shelf, usually looks whiter than the liquid beverages, and can taste fairly good. However, read the ingredients carefully. Like many liquid soymilks, dry soymilks contain sweeteners, thickeners, and flavorings. Some of them contain ingredients like hydrogenated oil and corn syrup rather than natural choices.

OTHER ASIAN SOYFOODS

There are foods used in various parts of Asia that you will find only in ethnic food stores and served in ethnic restaurants. Even in their native lands, they are not staples but are used as ingredients in certain dishes.

Okara

When soybeans are pressed to extract soymilk, the fibrous mass that remains is called *okara*. It has a mild, almost neutral flavor. Because of its porous texture, *okara* absorbs flavors easily. You may find *okara*, frozen, in some Japanese food stores. It is good added to baked items like cookies and muffins, in puddings, or scrambled with eggs. Natural food stores sell burgers made with *okara*.

Yuba

Only connoisseurs of Asian food and soy fans seem to know of this odd-sounding food. It is the skin that forms on the top of soymilk when it is heated, carefully lifted off, and set aside or dried. Fresh *yuba* is almost unknown in the U.S., though I have eaten it, in Chinatown, in an exquisite dish combined with fresh soybeans and salt-preserved vegetables. Usually, *yuba* is dried, forming thin, brittle, brown sheets that are soaked in water before using. If you have eaten vegetarian or mock duck at a Chinese restaurant, the thin, chewy sheets resembling soft phyllo enveloping the mushroom filling are *yuba*.

Kinoku

The Japanese make this fine, tan powder by grinding roasted soybeans. It has a strong taste similar to that of soy nuts. The Japanese and Chinese use it in sweets. My favorite way to eat it is mixed with sugar and sprinkled over brown rice or kasha. If you want to experiment with it, look for small bags of *kinoku* in Japanese food stores.

Natto

Made from fermented soybeans, this sticky, strong-tasting food has limited appeal to most Americans. It should not be confused with natto miso, a chunky, mildly sweet blend of soybeans, barley, *kombu* (a sea vegetable), and ginger. This miso makes a delicious condiment.

SECOND-GENERATION SOYFOODS

Most of the rapidly proliferating soyfood choices use highly refined forms of soy protein known as soy isolates and protein concentrates. These products are the result of intense industrial processing in which soybeans are defatted, ground into meal or flour, or rolled into flakes, then further processed to remove varying amounts of their carbohydrates and sugars.

In the defatting process, most companies use hexane, a petroleum derivative, as a solvent to help extract the oil from the soybeans. Presumably, all traces of this are gone by the time the defatted soy has been processed into isolate or protein concentrate.

Soy isolates and protein concentrates are mainly used as ingredients, though you may find them as a fine, fluffy powder in natural food stores. For home cooking, their use is limited to making drinks and mixing into recipes. Industrially used, they turn up in a dazzling array of products, natural and otherwise.

If you are passionate about eating whole foods and following a holistic diet, you probably prefer traditional soyfoods and products closest to them, like instant miso soup, smoked tofu, marinated tempeh burgers, and soy yogurt. If health benefits are the main reason drawing you to know soyfoods better, those with flavors and textures resembling what you are used to probably have more appeal. These are primarily the second-generation products. Although they use highly refined forms of soy, they contain all the potential health benefits you may be seeking. I also appreciate them for variety and convenience, especially when there's no time to cook.

Soy Dairy Products

The dairy and freezer cases in natural food stores are filled with soy products imitating dairy foods. You will find everything from milk and soy oil-based margarine to ice cream, yogurt, sour cream, cream cheese, and soy cheeses resembling mozzarella, Cheddar, Parmesan, American cheese, and more.

Soy dairy products are a boon to anyone who is lactose-intolerant, a growing problem in the United States because of our aging population and the increasing number of Asian-Americans. Like soymilk, other soy dairy products are cholesterol-free. While not necessarily lower in fat than their original counterparts, manufacturers are now making fat-reduced and fat-free soy dairy items too. Also, fortification with calcium and vitamins gives them the additional benefits of animal dairy products.

Although soy cheeses are lactose-free and contain no cholesterol, many contain oil. Only those made with casein, a cow's milk derivative, melt nicely. If you follow a vegan diet, these brands are unsuitable. When using soy cheese in recipes calling for shredded cheese, expect differences in texture as well as flavor compared to those made from animal milk. Personally, I find grated soy Parmesan cheese most closely resembles its animal counterpart; a boon in Italian cooking, it works equally well sprinkled on pastas and in making lasagna and other dishes. In recipes calling for grated Parmesan, you will notice that I suggest either the soy or cow's milk kind. Quite frankly, unless milk is forbidden to you, the flavor of true Parmigiano-Reggiano cheese is so unique and complex and adds so much to a dish, it is the one time that I will trade off the benefits of soy.

Soy Deli Foods

Why do people enjoy eating soy "meat" products? Mostly, the people who choose these hot dogs, deli slices, and ground meat replacers are in the process of giving up meat and want something familiar to take its place. They find it comforting to eat protein foods resembling the animal foods they are quitting.

Michael Cohen, an owner of Lightlife Foods, Inc.(a leading natural foods maker of both tempeh and high-tech natural meat alternatives), says vegetarian children like meat masqueraders because they feel they are eating the same foods as their friends who eat meat. Kids aged 11 and younger who eat meat, Cohen says, are not yet so used to its taste and texture that they mind the soy versions. Older children, like many adults, have less interest in these products because they are already used to the taste and texture of meat.

Meat-imitating soyfoods are hard to categorize because their "imitating" may be visual, textural, by taste, or some combination of these qualities. For example, frankfurters and patty-shaped tofu and tempeh burgers imitate meat mainly in shape. Some are precooked to a brown, meaty color for still greater visual resemblance. Many of the soy and wheat gluten cold cuts on the market also resemble deli foods visually, while imitating them poorly in other ways.

The degree to which soy can mimic the texture of meat—the fibrous, chewy texture of a hamburger or the nubbly, greasy feel of chopped meat—can be positively uncanny. Proving this, Boca Burger, the meatless burger brand that took first place in a *New York Times* survey, has a truly remarkable resemblance to the taste and texture of a real fast-food burger.

Meat replacers, like Gimme Lean™ from Lightlife, are meant to be used in recipes calling for ground meat. Like many veggie "meats," it is made from a combination of textured soy protein concentrate, soy isolate, and wheat gluten. It is fat-free—not the case with all meat alternatives. In a tasting I conducted, which included 12 cold cuts, 3 brands of hot dogs, and 10 kinds of sausage, Gimme Lean was the best-liked product. Indeed, it was the only product liked at all. Although soy hot dogs are fairly popular, as far as I am concerned, the less said about ersatz meats, the better.

Textured Vegetable Protein (TVP)

Despite its image as a downscale budget food, this is a soyfood worth exploring. The least heavily processed form of soy protein, virtually all TVP is made by Archer Daniels Midland (ADM), using defatted soy meal or flour. The flour is compressed and extruded under heat into flakes or chunks that look like something between toasted oatmeal and kibbled pet food. TVP is used both to replace meat and to extend it. Most TVP is used commercially. In home cooking, I like it in stews, chili, and stuffings. I think you will be pleased with the texture it gives them, the way it absorbs flavor, and the way it looks. Natural food stores sell TVP in bulk, usually in flakes. The best quality I have found comes from The Farm in Summertown, Tennessee.

Textured Soy Protein (TSP)

Another ADM product, TSP, is often confused with TVP because it is similar in appearance. TSP may cause less gastric distress than TVP, because this form of concentrated soy protein contains less oligosaccharides—the sugars in beans that tend to cause bloating and flatulence. The Farm in Summertown, Tennessee, is the best source for TSP. Few stores distinguish TSP from TVP, so you'll probably have a hard time finding out which you are getting.

Soy Isolate (Isolated Soy Protein)

Soy powders contain from 70 to 90 percent protein. Soy isolate, the most highly refined form of soy protein, is a white, almost tasteless, light powder that is 90 percent protein. It is a food so denatured that one hardly associates it with its source. Soy isolate is occasionally found in natural food stores. Mostly, it is used industrially as an ingredient in everything from meat products and meatless burgers to body-building drinks and dairy products. It is added because it improves texture as well as increasing the protein content of foods.

MORE SOY CHOICES

Often scorned or overlooked, just plain soybeans can be delectable. Boiled fresh soybeans, eaten as *edamame* by the Japanese, are irresistibly good. Dried black soybeans look and taste appealing cooked up and used in chili and soups. Roasted, rolled, and ground, soybeans are useful in various ways, from snacking to cooking and baking.

Fresh Soybeans

Some varieties of soybeans can be delicious if harvested when still immature. They arc bright green, while fully ripe soybeans are yellow. Simply boiled, these beans are sweet and tender, somewhat like a crunchy baby lima. For about three weeks in August, I can find fresh soybeans at the Greenmarket at Union Square in Manhattan. Separating the yellowish pods covered in brown fuzz from their straw-like stalks then shelling these beans is a lot of work, especially since most pods contain only two or three beans. Fortunately, there are simpler ways to enjoy fresh soybeans.

Japanese food stores sell bags of frozen *edamame*, which are green soybeans in their pods. Boil the beans in their shells in liberally salted water, then pop them from the pod right into your mouth, as the Japanese do. The Japanese eat *edamame* as a snack, usually with sake or beer. I like to keep a bowl on hand while I am working.

An American company, gambling that you will like fresh soybeans once you taste them, has trademarked the name Sweet Bean. Using this name, they have licensed Birds-Eye and Dean Foods to produce blends of frozen vegetables containing soybeans starting in fall of 1996. You can also find bags of shelled, frozen fresh soybeans at Asian food stores. I mix these protein- and fiber-rich beans with corn and combine them with other vegetables in soups and stir-fries.

Dried Black Soybeans

Dried soybeans are not usually worth bothering with. They take forever to cook, taste unpleasant, and have a tough, odd texture. Black soybeans are the exception, particularly a variety called Black Jet, which I usually order from Canada (see "Mail Order Sources"). These have a definite yet mild soy flavor, a pleasant sweetness, and a texture that works well in many dishes. Shiloh Farms and Nesheminy Valley, two major natural food distributors, sell 1-pound bags of dried black soybeans to natural food stores. These beans take two to three hours to prepare (one and a half hours in a pressure cooker), even when they have soaked for 24 hours. In Japan, black soybeans are prized for medicinal purposes. And in case you wondered, the fermented black beans used in Chinese cooking are black soybeans.

Soy Flour

Soy flour is made from whole soybeans that are hulled, split, roasted, and ground. Sometimes it is made from defatted beans. Soy flour is pale beige and has a strong bean taste. Primarily, it is useful to boost the protein content in baked items. It also helps to make baked goods more moist. This flour contains no gluten. Because of its strong taste and gritty texture, a little soy flour goes a long way. Most natural food stores carry it.

Soy Grits

I find it hard to say anything good about these coarsely ground dried soybeans. They take a long time to cook and have a strong flavor that few people like. Cook soy grits at least 30 minutes longer than usual if they are not made from recently harvested beans. Because they need to cook so long, it's hard to combine them with corn, barley, or other kinds of grits.

Soy Flakes

These golden flakes look like large, thick rolled oats. They are usually made from hulled soybeans and have a strong soy taste. The good news is that hulling removes much of the fat from soy flakes. The bad news is their taste and texture—this is another soyfood that I recommend avoiding.

Soy Nuts

Quite the rage at one point, soy nuts are roasted split soybeans. They have a strong taste and dry crunch that you will either enjoy or wish to avoid. Since soybeans are a rich source of protein and oil, ½ cup of dry roasted soy nuts provides a substantial 34 grams of protein along with 18.6 grams of fat. Use them as a quick, high-nutrient snack, but try to keep the munching to one handful at a sitting.

COOKING WITH SOYFOODS

Many people have cooked with tofu at some point, probably cubed and added to a stir-fry or pureed to use in a dip. Before you explore the wider world of soy cooking opened up by the recipes in the following chapters, here is information about how to buy, store, and use various soyfoods. Read it before going on to the recipes. It will help you understand the versatility of soy and how to make it work for you. This information is important, because soyfoods, especially tofu and soymilk, vary so much in texture and density from brand to brand.

Tofu

I divide the uses of tofu between cooking it and cooking with it. Recipes for cooking it mostly combine bean curd with highly flavored ingredients through marinating, braising, or stir-frying. Techniques for cooking with tofu include methods that significantly alter its texture as well as transforming its taste: pressing, freezing, frying, and pureeing. Sautéing and grilling fall into this category, too.

When artfully blended into savory recipes, cooking with tofu is sensually as well as nutritionally rewarding. It can give soups a creamy quality and enrich pureed vegetables as well as making a good base for dips and dressings, without adding the characteristic flat, bland, or chalky flavor that bothers many people.

One way to minimize or even avoid that "tofu taste" is by adding a bit of fresh lemon juice. Somehow, this counteracts any blah quality in a way that not even salt or strong seasonings can. This brightening touch of lemon juice makes a difference even in desserts like tofu chocolate mousse and cheesecake.

Before getting into techniques, it helps to get familiar with variable factors in cooking with tofu. For example, you probably have noted that tofu comes in a range of densities. Each one—soft, medium, firm, and extra firm—varies from one brand to another. To further complicate your soy shopping, the texture, which can be critical in a recipe, will be different with regular, reduced-fat, and low-fat bean curd from the same manufacturer. With a few tries, you will quickly know which products you like and which work best in different dishes. Just be sure, when you experiment, to disregard the way manufacturers categorize their tofu and see how you would describe it. Once you do this, you'll know just what brand and density to reach for at the store when making a dip, a stir-fry, or a cheesecake.

Tofu comes in packages containing 16 ounces, 10½ ounces, 10 ounces, 8 ounces, 7 ounces, and 6 ounces, so look carefully when you grab a package at the store. Mostly, regular bean curd will be 16 or 8 ounces; silken tofu, 10½ ounces; and baked or smoked bean curd, 7 or 6 ounces, but better to check and be safe than sorry. Some of the tubs that look like they will be 16 ounces are shallower and only hold 10 ounces.

One more thing before getting into cooking. Prices vary greatly for tofu. In New York City supermarkets, I have seen tofu for as much as $2.79 for 16 ounces. That seems reasonable for four to eight servings of a high-quality protein made with pure ingredients. But why pay it when natural food stores usually charge as little as $1.29? (If you freeze tofu, it's always possible to take advantage of the specials occasionally offered.) Also, locally produced brands may be less expensive. But I find the best prices at Asian markets. For example, Mori-Nu that costs up to $1.79 for a 10½-ounce box, can be $0.89 at the Japanese grocer near me. And while I would not go to Chinatown just to save money on tofu, it is an opportunity to enjoy fresh tofu, which costs about $1 for a pint container. (Look for this warm, delicate, custard-like bean curd at shops that make tofu.)

Pressing   Pressing increases the density of tofu, giving it a smoother texture. Most people prefer pressed tofu. Even extra firm tofu has excess water, which pressing removes. This is also a good way to compact soft tofu when you want something denser.

Place one 16-ounce block of firm or extra firm tofu on your work surface. Holding a sharp knife parallel to the work surface, slice the bean curd in half, making two slabs, each about 1-inch thick.

On a cutting board big enough to hold the two pieces of tofu side by side, place a piece of foil larger than the area the bean curd will cover. Center the tofu on the foil. Place the board with its side over the edge of the sink. Slip a book under the edge of the board away from the sink, raising the board to about a 15-degree angle. This helps the water pressed from the tofu to drain.

Cover the bean curd with another piece of foil. Place a second cutting board or flat, heavy object like a book on top of the foil. Add weight until the sides of the tofu bulge slightly. Be particularly attentive when pressing soft tofu. You can add more weight after a while, but too much at the beginning can make it split.

Distributing the weight evenly assures that the tofu is evenly pressed. I have three cast-iron skillets that I place in a nest on top of a thick book. Let the tofu, weighted, sit for 30 minutes. Check to see if it is firm enough. If not, replace the weight and press for an additional 15 to 30 minutes. Should the tofu come out wedge-shaped, redistribute the weight and repeat the process until the thickness of the bean curd evens out.

If the angle of this Rube Goldberg set-up seems too precarious, leave the bottom board flat on the counter and use a towel to mop up the water pressed from the tofu.

You can press tofu ahead of time, then submerge it in a pan of water and refrigerate until ready to use. It keeps two to three days. Be sure to change the water daily.

Some books advise wrapping tofu in paper towels before pressing it. I find that the towels become soaked quickly and I end up changing them several times, which seems wasteful. And I don't like the thought that chemicals used in the paper might possibly leach into the tofu.

Freezing   Freezing gives bean curd a dry, chicken-like texture and makes it particularly receptive to marinades and sauces. This is also a way to store bean curd for months. Use defrosted tofu the same way as cubed tofu or crumble it over salads and into soups and stews. Any bean curd can be frozen, though pressed firm and extra firm regular tofu work best.

Using 16 ounces of firm or extra firm tofu pressed in two slabs, place the tofu, uncovered, on a baking rack and put it in the freezer. If possible, turn the temperature to the coldest setting so the bean curd freezes as quickly as possible. Look for the tofu to darken to yellow or even amber after about 48 hours.

Frozen tofu may be defrosted after 24 hours, but storing it longer improves it, up to about one week. After that, wrap the unused frozen tofu in plastic; it keeps for several months.

To defrost, set a block of frozen tofu in a large bowl. Pour 2 to 3 quarts of boiling water over the bean curd. Let it sit in the water five to ten minutes, just until defrosted. As large slabs soften, break them into smaller pieces or slice them to hasten the process. As soon as the tofu is defrosted, pour off the water. Immediately refill the bowl with cool or cold water. One piece at a time, gently press the bean curd between your palms to squeeze out the water; squeezing too hard makes the tofu crumble into curd-like bits, while the right amount of pressure molds the tofu into cutlet-like pieces. Use according to recipe directions.

Marinating Marinating can be done three ways. Marinating in liquid is most effective when the tofu is cooked in the mixture either by simmering or baking, then cooling the bean curd in the marinade. At least start with a hot marinade, as Green's, the great San Francisco vegetarian restaurant, does when preparing tofu for its zesty sandwich and brochettes. Marinades work on any kind of tofu, though they penetrate best on pressed firm or extra firm.

Coating tofu with a highly flavored paste made with pureed ingredients also works nicely. Good bases for a marinating paste include mustard, peanut butter, miso, or pureed aromatics such as onions, garlic, ginger, and herbs. This is also an effective way to use chile peppers to flavor tofu.

Dry rubs are not very successful on bean curd. They don't penetrate the density of pressed tofu, while the water in unpressed bean curd dilutes them. Also, dry rubs tend to char during grilling, turning bitter, or to dissolve into the liquid in wet cooking.

Sautéing and Pan-crisping   I sauté a whole pound of tofu using as little as 1 to 2 tablespoons of oil. Sautéing seals, colors, and crisps the outside while leaving the center of the bean curd soft and creamy. This contrast can be most appealing. Sauté cubed tofu before adding it to stews, casseroles, or soups.

Pan-crisping or pan-frying is simply browning tofu in about $\frac{1}{2}$ inch of oil. This process makes the tofu more chewy. It becomes slightly spongy and eager to soak up sauces. Pan-crisped bean curd can be refrigerated for a day or two. It is particularly good in stir-fries and casseroles.

Frying   Frying gives tofu a crisp texture all the way through and an attractive golden color. Cubes of deep-fried tofu can be added to a stir-fry or served on a bed of rice, topped with a sauce. Battering tofu, then dredging it in bread crumbs before frying, makes nuggets that are seductively crisp outside and succulent inside.

Braising   Simmer cubed tofu gently in a highly flavored liquid, and the taste will penetrate entirely through the bean curd in as little as 20 minutes. Braising gives strong flavor and firms the texture. Red-cooking, the Asian technique that uses a soy-seasoned liquid often flavored with star anise, is an increasingly popular form of braising. It imparts dark, rich color and very intense flavor.

Braising can be done on top of the stove or in the oven. If you braise tofu until most of the liquid has evaporated, the bean curd will be firmer when it cools. Braising works well with pressed or frozen regular tofu. It does not work well with silken bean curd. If you find tofu too bland, braise it in strong vegetable broth or apple juice or red-cook it before adding to a stir-fry.

Pureeing Any tofu can be pureed in a blender or the food processor. Use silken or soft regular tofu for dressings, sauces, cream soups, puddings, and creamy cheesecake. Firmer tofu makes thicker dips and denser, quiche-type dishes.

Parboiling Some Asian recipes call for parboiling tofu, a process that milds down the flavor. This a good solution if you don't like the taste of tofu you've bought. This process is also useful when bean curd tastes sourish—more likely a sign of age than of spoilage. Simply cook the bean curd in boiling water along with a pinch of salt for five to ten minutes, depending on the size of the pieces of tofu. Refreshing bean curd this way also firms it a bit. This can be useful if a recipe calls for tofu more solid than what you have on hand.

Storing and Handling Tofu Tofu sold in a tub or pouch can be stored in its sealed container until you use it. However, it is better to open the package, discard the liquid, and pour fresh water into the tub. Keeping tofu this way maintains a fresher flavor, which is worth the bother of having to change the water daily. Tofu stored this way may still last up to ten days, depending on how fresh it was when you bought it.

Tofu is a perishable food. Treat it like dairy and meat products unless it is in a shelf-stable aseptic package. When buying tofu, check the expiration date on the package and pick packages with the furthest date. Refrigerate bean curd as soon as you get it home.

Few people realize that, as with animal foods, tofu is susceptible to unfriendly bacteria, including salmonella. Handle it as you would raw poultry or meat. This means you should wash work surfaces and your hands before touching the bean curd. When marinating tofu, setting it in the refrigerator is wise.

If you want to eat tofu often, it pays to develop a repertoire of recipes that use it with a light hand as well as serving dishes that feature it. For example, in place of olive oil, try adding a couple of ounces of pureed tofu—and that dash of lemon juice—to mashed potatoes. Or crumble some frozen tofu into a pot of chili. It will seem to disappear as it soaks up flavor, but the addition will still benefit your family nutritionally. After all, a serving of tofu a day . . .

Miso

I suggest keeping on hand three kinds of miso. They should include a tub of sweet white or chickpea miso, a mild brown rice or barley (mugi) miso, and a meaty hatcho miso. Use the light miso for making dressings and spreads, the darker, more salty ones for enhancing the flavors in soups and stews. You may even want to combine two kinds. This is done in Japanese cooking. The owner of Fuji, the oldest Japanese restaurant in New York City, taught me to make miso soup by blending equal parts of a sweet and a dark miso.

Properly stored, even unpasteurized miso keeps for months. I've kept dark varieties for over a year. The best way to store every kind of miso is to transfer it into a tightly covered glass jar and keep it in the refrigerator. Use a clean utensil when scooping out a portion.

You don't need to use Japanese recipes to enjoy miso. With all the fusion cooking going on, you'll find new recipes and myriad ways to incorporate this savory bean paste into your own favorite dishes—perhaps using it in place of soy sauce in some instances.

Among the ingredients in Western cooking, miso seems to have an affinity for beans, all kinds of winter squash, eggplant, and dishes containing tomatoes. Miso can also take the place of dairy, particularly in soups and dressings. Try it mashed into root vegetables in place of butter (it doesn't taste like dairy, but it provides the same kind of rich flavor and creamy texture).

When cooking with miso, it is easy to go overboard. I suggest a 1:4 ratio, that is, 1 tablespoon of miso to 4 cups of liquid or 4 servings of food. No matter what, I rarely use more than 2 tablespoons of miso in a recipe.

For hot dishes, add miso at the end of cooking time. Boiling it and prolonged exposure to heat kill the live bacteria in miso and diminish its rich aroma. Take care not to boil a dish containing miso when reheating it.

Always blend miso with a bit of liquid before adding it to a dish. Bill Shurtleff calls this "creaming." Thinning out the miso in this way assures that it won't break up into tiny bits that stubbornly refuse to dissolve, especially in hot dishes. The easiest way to cream miso is to dip 2 to 4 tablespoons of liquid from the pot, blend it with the miso in a small bowl, then stir this mixture back into the pot. For cold uses like salad dressing, combine the miso with the vinegar or other liquids. You can also cream miso by mashing it in a *suribachi*, a Japanese mortar lined with fine ridges. This technique is most useful for breaking up chunky miso.

Tempeh

Usually, tempeh is steamed or fried before it is added to a dish. Steaming makes it taste milder and gives the tempeh a creamy texture. Frying tempeh or just browning it in a pan sprayed with nonstick cooking spray adds appealing color and crispness that remain even after it has been immersed in stew or soup. As I have mentioned, tempeh marinates beautifully.

Buy tempeh that is firm and looks nicely veined with white mycelium. If you see black patches, do not worry. It runs counter to everything you know about food, but with tempeh, black mold simply indicates the bacteria in it are still active. It is not spoiled. Just trim that part away and proceed to cook the tempeh, unless it feels slimy or smells of ammonia.

Soymilk

Soymilk is wonderfully adaptable in cooking. I use it in all kinds of desserts, from puddings to crème anglaise and pastry cream. For savory dishes, I am more conservative because of the sweetness and sometimes the strong bean taste of some soymilk. Still, this dairy-free food can be excellent for sauces, gravies, and some soups.

When cooking with soymilk, the main concerns are selecting a brand and type with the right texture for your recipe and picking one whose color will not diminish the appearance of the finished dish.

A number of soymilks are grayish or tan-colored. Also, heat from prolonged cooking darkens the color of some soymilk. This can be unappealing in certain soups, sauces, or desserts. To counter this characteristic, think about using soymilk in recipes calling for chocolate, cinnamon, or pumpkin and for making pastry cream to fill into pastries or fruit. Less sweetened soymilks also work in savory dishes calling for highly colored vegetables like carrots, broccoli, and red pepper.

As far as texture is concerned, the less fat, the thinner the soymilk. To pour over cereal, go as lean as you wish, but for cooking I suggest "whole" soymilk. Even EdenSoy, for example, contains 4 grams of fat per 8 ounces, which is the amount of fat you get in a cup of cow's milk. And to repeat: While you should keep total fat consumption in hand, these are unsaturated, cholesterol-free lipids. Because the milky texture in soymilk comes from thickeners, I find some brands troublesome for certain uses. So far, I cannot get Silk, the fresh soymilk, to thicken in puddings cooked on the stove or to set in the oven, no matter what I use with it, from cornstarch to eggs. Since I like the texture of this product, I am continuing to work on this challenge.

Other Soy Dairy Foods

Not all soy-based dairy products work as well in cooking as soymilk tends to. For example, soy sour cream, remarkable for use in dips and dolloped into soups, does not work in baking or sauce-making; the gums that hold it together do not stand up to that kind of cooking. Soy yogurt is another dairy product bound together with natural gums that are not suited to cooking (the murky color of unflavored soy yogurt can also pose a problem, except in dips). Soy-based cream cheese, on the other hand, makes stunning cheesecakes. My advice when you want to cook with soy dairy products is to look for recipes from the manufacturer and in soyfoods cookbooks. When adapting your own recipes to use soy, be prepared to experiment and adjust.

A reminder: Soy dairy products are as perishable as those made with animal milk. Look at expiration dates on packaging. When possible, buy items a week or more before their expiration date. Refrigerate and treat these foods with the same care as conventional dairy foods.

COOK'S NOTES

Although cooking is based on traditional techniques, it is also influenced by individual preferences. Here are some ingredients and ways of doing things that I favor.

For example, I use organic ingredients as much as possible. That includes not simply grains and beans, fresh fruits and vegetables, but other items, too, as indicated below.

Herbs, Spices, and Flavorings

Use fresh herbs whenever possible. When they are not at hand, I also use dried herbs. Since it's easy to overdo it with dried herbs, the recipes in this book provide the quantities I recommend. Because they lose flavor and aroma, especially in the heat of the kitchen, I replace unused dried herbs after six months.

The sweet, or baking, spices—cinnamon, allspice, ground clove, and the like, seem to hold up better than dried herbs. Nutmeg should be grated fresh; it makes a world of difference in flavor. (Cookware stores sell little nutmeg graters. The whole nuts keep for ages.) Ground cumin quickly loses its strength and should be replaced as often as dried herbs. Paprika keeps well if refrigerated. (Do buy a good quality, like The Pride of Szeged, in the red can, imported from Hungary.)

Freshness counts for pepper, too. I use only freshly ground pepper. Since there is a pronounced difference in flavor between black and white pepper, I keep a separate mill for each, choosing which to use depending on the dish.

For freshness and flavor, the spices, herbs, and vanilla extract from Penzey's Spice House are exceptional. Penzey's claims to grind and blend their offerings every week. If you require seasonings that are not irradiated or fumigated, Frontier Herbs offers herbs and spices in bulk and in individual, sealed jars. Look for them in natural food stores.

Salt is another matter of personal choice. I use coarse-grained Kosher salt, which is milder than sea salt. If you use sea salt, adjust to taste accordingly.

Nuts

The fresher the better. At farmer's markets around San Francisco, I have bought freshly harvested walnuts. Their flavor is incredible compared to what you buy in bags at the supermarket. To assure freshness, buy small amounts that will be used up quickly. Store unused nuts sealed in a jar in the freezer.

Almonds are a snap to peel, and doing so saves you the cost of buying blanched almonds. Simply throw whole almonds in boiling water for 1 to 2 minutes. Remove with a slotted spoon. Pinch the pointed end with your nail and squeeze the rounded end with your fingers. Out will pop the almond. Let the blanched nuts dry for 15 to 20 minutes before using or storing them in the freezer.

Oils

I use two oils constantly—namely olive oil and canola oil. Olive oil adds flavor. Use extra virgin olive oil as much as you can afford to. In particular, I use two Spanish olive oils. For cooking, I like L'Estornell's organic extra virgin olive oil, which has a medium strength and full flavor. For salads and more special occasions, I use Nunez de Prado. This is a limited-production oil that is intense without the bitter aftertaste or harsh burn of some Italian extra virgin olive oils. Overall, I find Spanish olive oils compare in quality to most Italian oils, at a better price.

For cooking where a neutral-tasting oil is called for, I favor canola oil. Look for cold-pressed or expeller-expressed brands. These are produced without heating and denaturing.

Storing oil properly is important. Oils begin to oxidize long before they taste rancid. I store oil in the refrigerator, which protects it from heat and light, both of which accelerate its breakdown. When you have used a quarter to a third of the bottle, if possible, transfer the oil to a smaller container so there is less air to oxidize it. If keeping oil on the shelf, try to store it in colored bottles that shield it from light. Never keep it near the heat of the stove.

I find one tablespoon sufficient for most sautéing, so oil lasts a long time in my kitchen. Normally, I pour about 2 ounces into a dark glass bottle and keep that out, storing the rest in the refrigerator. When the small bottle is empty, I wash it out and refill it.

Produce

When possible, I buy produce from local farmers at the farmer's markets set up in New York City several times a week. (Locally, they are called Greenmarkets.) Otherwise, I shop at natural food stores.

Carrots—I only peel carrots for a fancy dinner. I do this because my mother always told me that the skin contains many vitamins; I also do it to save time.

Potatoes—If the potatoes are sprayed, I peel them before cooking. If they're organic, I boil them in their skin, then use the cooking liquid when making vegetable broth.

Mushrooms—Peeling mushrooms irks me. Wiping them with a damp towel seems to do the job, especially since most white mushrooms are grown in a sterile medium. I don't mind slightly shriveled mushrooms; their more concentrated flavor works well in most dishes.

Garlic—Roast a whole head or two of garlic at a time. To do this, I cut each off horizontally, about ½ inch below the top, exposing the tops of all the cloves. Preheat the oven to 400 degrees. Rub each head of garlic with 1 teaspoon olive oil. Seal the heads in foil. Bake until the garlic is soft when poked, 40 to 50 minutes. Let cool. Wrapped in foil, roasted garlic keeps three to four days in the refrigerator. To use, squeeze out the creamy garlic cocooned in the compartments of the flower-like head until you have the desired amount.

Peppers—Roasting fresh sweet peppers is absolutely worth the effort. On a gas stove, sit them on the burner over a high flame. As they char, use long tongs to turn them until the peppers are nicely blackened all over. Start with peppers at room temperature and this takes about 10 minutes. Seal the charred peppers in a paper bag for 20 minutes (up to an hour). Peel them with your fingers. Do not rinse them. A few bits of charred skin clinging to the peppers matter less than the flavor you will lose. When seeding the peppers, be sure to capture their flavorful juice by holding them over a bowl.

Stock

In meatless cooking, where you need all the flavor you can get, making stock from vegetable parings is commendable but time consuming. And who's got room to store it? Avoid broths where the flavor is dominated by cabbage, broccoli, or other strong-tasting additions. Recently, a great choice became available that makes using vegetable broth a snap. It is the canned vegetable broth made by Arrowhead Mills. I confess that I created this product for the company, but I did it as much to make it easy to have on hand what I really wanted for cooking as to benefit professionally from this product.

Other instant vegetable broths I recommend are a concentrated paste in a jar from The Organic Gourmet and Powder Vegetable Broth Mix in a small canister from Morga. Both are imported from Europe, and therefore pricey, but a little goes a long way. Any of these instant vegetable broths give soups, cooked grains, and other dishes a flavor lift.

Sweeteners

I generally use Florida Crystals in place of white sugar. Produced in Florida from locally grown sugar cane, it will soon be available organically grown. Generically, this sweetener is known as unbleached cane sugar. It dissolves as well as regular sugar in most cooking and baking, but retains some of the minerals removed from white sugar. When brown sugar is called for, you can also use

Succanat, an even less refined form of cane sugar. Dark brown, it tastes faintly like molasses—a benefit in some recipes. Maple syrup is perhaps my favorite sweetener. Dark, thick grade B has more pronounced flavor and costs less than the fancier, lighter grade A. Some natural food stores sell it in bulk.

SOUPS, APPETIZERS, AND FIRST COURSES

SOUPS, APPETIZERS, AND FIRST COURSES

*my favorite recipes

Broccoli Bisque

YIELD: 6 SERVINGS

The inspiration for this soup came from Michael's Nook, an elegant country hotel in the English Lake District. Broccoli and spinach give the soup an intense flavor. Pureeing in the blender makes it velvety smooth; puree it in a food processor if you prefer a bit of texture. Garlic Tempeh Croutons (page 170) make a nice garnish.

1 tablespoon canola oil
1 medium onion, chopped
1 large clove garlic, minced
¾ pound broccoli florets (about 1 bunch)
4 cups vegetable stock or water
½ pound fresh spinach, stemmed and washed, or 5 ounces
    (½ package) frozen spinach, defrosted and squeezed dry
8 ounces soft regular or silken tofu, cubed
¼ teaspoon red pepper flakes
½ teaspoon ground cumin
½ teaspoon dried oregano
1 teaspoon salt
½ teaspoon freshly ground pepper
Juice of 1 lime

1 In a large saucepan, heat the oil. Sauté the onion and garlic until the onions are soft, about 8 minutes. Add the broccoli and stock. Cook, covered, until the broccoli is soft, about 15 minutes.

2 Add the spinach, tofu, pepper flakes, cumin, oregano, salt, and pepper. Cover and simmer 10 minutes.

3 In a food processor or blender, puree the soup, in 2 batches if necessary.

4 Just before serving, stir in the lime juice. Check the seasoning and adjust to taste.

VARIATION

This soup can also be served chilled. As a garnish, toasted dehydrated onion flakes complement the cold soup nicely. The sweet and slightly sharp flavor of the crisped flakes is perfect with the chilled soup. Simply roast 2 tablespoons of the flakes in a small, dry skillet until they turn golden-brown, stirring constantly, about 4 minutes. Take care, as they will burn very quickly.

Corn and Smoked Tofu Chowder

YIELD: 4 SERVINGS

Smoked tofu has a firm texture and appealing aroma. It adds pronounced flavor to any dish. Here it stands in perfectly for the bacon traditionally used in chowder. Enjoy this light soup in warm weather—usually the time of year when the best fresh corn is in season. Slightly undercook the vegetables, as they will remain pleasantly firm when the chowder is reheated.

1 tablespoon canola oil
1 small red onion, finely chopped
1 large rib celery, finely chopped
2 cups light vegetable broth
1 medium potato, peeled, cut in ¾-inch cubes
1 teaspoon thyme leaves, or ½ teaspoon dried thyme
1 cup smoked tofu, cut in ½-inch cubes
1 cup fresh corn kernels or defrosted frozen corn
1 cup plain regular soymilk
Salt and freshly ground pepper
2 tablespoons minced dill or snipped chives

1 In a large saucepan, heat the oil over medium-high heat. Add the onion and celery and sauté until translucent, about 5 minutes, stirring occasionally.

2 Pour in the broth and bring to a boil. Add the potato. When the pot returns to a boil, reduce the heat. Add the thyme and simmer until the potato is slightly underdone, about 15 minutes.

3 Add the tofu and corn. Raise the heat until the soup bubbles gently. Mix in the soymilk. When heated through, season the soup to taste with salt and pepper. Ladle the chowder into bowls. Garnish with the dill or chives and serve.

VARIATION

Instead of the soymilk and vegetable broth, I sometimes use bottled clam juice. If you are not strictly vegetarian, this makes for a seafood chowder that is rich yet light.

Miso Onion Soup

YIELD: 4 SERVINGS

If you love French onion soup, try this simplified version. It provides the many virtues of miso soup plus added flavor from the ginger and sautéed onion.

1 teaspoon canola oil
1 clove garlic, crushed
1 small onion, sliced lengthwise into thin crescents
½ teaspoon finely minced ginger root
2 tablespoons sweet white miso
2 tablespoons red or barley miso
1 scallion, white and green part, thinly sliced

1 In a medium saucepan, heat the oil over medium heat. Add the garlic and sauté 30 seconds, just until the garlic is fragrant. Add the onion and sauté until very soft, about 5 minutes, taking care not to let it color.

2 Add 4 cups water and bring to a boil. Reduce the heat, cover the pot, and simmer 3 minutes. Add the ginger.

3 Place the white and red misos in a small bowl. Spoon ¼ cup of the liquid from the pot into the bowl. Blend the miso with the liquid to make a creamy mixture. Stir this mixture into the pot. Bring the soup to just below a boil. Ladle the soup into bowls, garnish with a few of the scallion slices, and serve immediately.

VARIATION

For a light meal in a bowl, add cubes of silken tofu to each serving of this soup. For a more substantial meal, add cooked *udon*, the chubby, white Japanese noodles.

Ginger Carrot Soup

YIELD: 4 SERVINGS

The silken texture, appealing color, and mouth-filling flavor of this soup will make you purr with satisfaction. Use organic carrots, unpeeled—this not only adds nutritional goodness, but it also saves time. Present this soup for the first course of a special dinner or make it the center of a light meal, accompanied by a green salad and crusty bread.

1 tablespoon canola oil
⅓ cup chopped onion
3 cups sliced carrots
1½ teaspoons minced ginger root
2 tablespoons minced shallots
2 cups vegetable broth
1 cup plain regular soymilk
1 teaspoon tamari
Salt and freshly ground pepper
2 tablespoons chopped fresh coriander

1 In a large saucepan, heat the oil over medium-high heat. Add the onion, carrots, ginger, and shallots. Sauté until the onion is translucent, about 5 minutes, stirring often.

2 Add the broth and bring to a boil. Cover tightly and simmer until the carrots are very soft, 35 to 40 minutes.

3 With a slotted spoon, transfer the carrots to a blender. Add half the cooking liquid from the carrots, soymilk, and tamari. Process until the carrots are pureed. For a thinner soup, blend in additional vegetable broth or soymilk. Season to taste with salt and pepper. Pour the hot soup into serving bowls and garnish with the chopped coriander.

VARIATIONS

Try using 2 cups of sliced carrots and 1 cup of diced, peeled sweet potato or yam. For a different variation, butternut squash works nicely in place of the carrots, particularly when combined with some apple. I use 2 cups of squash and 1 cup of diced Sweet Golden Delicious apples.

Sweet Pea and Coriander Potage

YIELD: 4 SERVINGS

The vernal color of this soup tells you it is special. Your first taste proves this blending of sweet peas with fresh coriander is a felicitous marriage. This soup cooks in just 20 minutes. It also keeps well overnight and reheats beautifully.

1 tablespoon canola oil
1 medium onion, chopped (about 1 cup)
1 cup chopped celery
2 cloves garlic, minced
1 teaspoon grated ginger root
2 cups vegetable broth or water
1 (10-ounce) package frozen baby green peas
1½ cups plain regular soymilk
½ cup fresh coriander leaves, loosely packed
Salt and freshly ground pepper

1 In a medium saucepan, heat the oil over medium-high heat. Sauté the onion, celery, garlic, and ginger until the onion is translucent, about 5 minutes.

2 Add the broth. Bring the soup to a simmer and cook, uncovered, 10 minutes, until the celery is almost soft.

3 Add the frozen peas and cook until they are heated through, about 5 minutes. Mix in the soymilk and coriander.

4 In a food processor, puree the soup, in 2 batches if necessary. Season to taste with salt and pepper and serve.

VARIATION

This soup can also be served chilled. When served cold, stir in 2 teaspoons lime juice along with the salt and pepper.

Korean Pine Nut Soup

YIELD: 3 SERVINGS

Koreans consider this creamy soup comfort food. They enjoy it as a homemade treat, a light meal, or to nourish themselves when feeling poorly. To this soup, which is essentially a nut milk thickened with rice, I add *kinoku* (Japanese roasted soy flour), which further enriches the flavor. *Kinoku* is sold at all Japanese and most other Asian food stores; if it is not available, *tahini* can take its place. This soup works well as a light meal or an elegant first course.

2 tablespoons arborio rice
½ cup pine nuts (about 2½ ounces; see note)
1 cup plain regular soymilk
1 tablespoon *kinoku*
½ teaspoon unbleached cane sugar
2 medium dried dates, pitted and chopped

NOTE

Pine nuts grown around the Mediterranean cost several times more than those from Asia, but their flavor is sweeter and milder, without the bitter taste found in Asian pine nuts. The Mediterranean nuts are more evenly shaped, rather like a plump, beige rice grain. Those from Asia are broader at one end and rather triangular in shape. Pine nuts easily turn rancid, so be sure the ones you are getting are fresh.

1 In a small saucepan, combine the rice with 1 cup cold water. Cover, bring to a boil, reduce the heat, and simmer 20 minutes, until the rice is very soft. Let the rice sit, covered, until ready to use.

2 In a blender, puree the nuts with ½ cup water. Add another ½ cup water and continue blending until the nuts are finely pureed. Blend in the soymilk.

3 Pour the nut milk through a fine strainer, pressing lightly on the solids to extract more of the liquid. Rinse and dry the blender container. Return the strained nut milk to the blender. Add the cooked rice, *kinoku*, and sugar. Blend until the soup is smooth.

4 Pour the soup into a medium saucepan and heat, taking care not to let it boil. Ladle the hot soup into 3 small bowls. Garnish each bowl with a third of the chopped dates and serve.

VARIATION

You can turn this soup into a dessert by using 1 cup plain regular soymilk in place of the water when processing the nuts.

Roasted Vegetable Stock

YIELD: ABOUT 6 CUPS

Roasting the vegetables caramelizes their natural sugars, adding intensity and body to the flavor of this stock. It is a perfect base for hearty soups, stews, and chili. My friend Dalia Carmel insisted that I include celery root in this stock. It adds wonderful flavor (thank you, Dalia).

2 medium carrots, coarsely chopped
2 medium leeks, white and light green portions, coarsely chopped
1 large onion, coarsely chopped
1 white turnip, coarsely chopped
1 medium zucchini, coarsely chopped
1 cup coarsely chopped, peeled celery root
2 tablespoons canola oil
12 parsley stems
2 bay leaves

1 Preheat the oven to 425 degrees.

2 Place the carrots, leeks, onion, turnip, zucchini, and celery root in a large roasting pan. Drizzle the oil over the vegetables. With your hands, rub the oil over the vegetables until they are coated all over.

3 Roast the vegetables until they are browned, about 55 minutes, stirring 2 to 3 times to help them color evenly and to avoid burning.

4 Transfer the roasted vegetables to a large, deep pot. Add the parsley stems, bay leaves, and 12 cups (3 quarts) cold water. Over high heat, bring the broth just to a boil. Reduce the heat and simmer gently for 2 hours; the liquid will be reduced almost by half. Let the stock cool to room temperature in the pot.

5 Strain the stock into a large bowl. Using a slotted spoon, transfer the vegetables in batches into a strainer. Holding the strainer over the bowl of stock, press on the vegetables with the back of the spoon to extract more of their juices. (Press lightly—too much pressure will push bits of vegetable through the strainer, making the stock cloudy.) Ladle the stock into clean containers. Cover tightly and refrigerate or freeze. This stock keeps 2 to 3 days in the refrigerator, or up to 3 months in the freezer.

VARIATION

For a bit of zip, include a dried chile pepper. Use this version for making chili and cooking beans.

Carrot Pâté

YIELD: 2 CUPS

Spread this moist, nutty pâté on crackers or stuff it into celery sticks. You can also serve this bright and brightly flavored spread as a first course, mounded on a bed of romaine lettuce and watercress.

1 tablespoon extra virgin olive oil
1 small onion, finely chopped
3 medium carrots (about ½ pound), thinly sliced
¼ cup orange juice
2 (2-inch) strips orange zest
½ teaspoon ground coriander
⅛ teaspoon freshly ground nutmeg
¼ teaspoon freshly ground pepper
4 ounces firm regular tofu
1 tablespoon mellow miso
½ cup walnuts

1 In a medium skillet with a tight-fitting cover, heat the oil over medium-high heat. Sauté the onion and carrots until the onion is soft, about 8 minutes, taking care not to let the onion brown. (It will take on a golden color because of the carotene in the carrots.)

2 Add the orange juice, orange zest, coriander, nutmeg, and pepper. Stir in ¼ cup water. Cover, reduce the heat, and simmer until the carrots are soft, about 12 minutes. Uncover and continue cooking until nearly all the liquid has evaporated from the pan.

3 Transfer the cooked carrots to the bowl of a food processor. Process until they are finely chopped. Crumble the tofu into 3 or 4 pieces and add to the carrots. Process until the tofu and carrots are well blended. Add the miso and process to blend. Add the walnuts. Let the food processor run until the pâté is almost creamy, with just a bit of texture from the nuts and carrot, 1 to 2 minutes. Scrape the pâté into a small bowl. Cover and refrigerate for 1 hour to allow the flavors to meld. This spread keeps 1 to 2 days, although it loses some flavor after about 8 hours.

VARIATION

Use soft regular tofu instead of firm to make a creamy, thick puree that works beautifully as a salad dressing over crisp greens.

Sun-Dried Tomato Dip

YIELD: 2 CUPS

Once you taste this dip, don't be surprised if you find your-
self eating it with everything, from celery sticks to rice cakes
to scrambled eggs. Take time to roast the red peppers your-
self (see below); the flavor will be truly superior to the ones
from a jar. Chipotle chiles (jalapeño peppers allowed to ripen
until red and then smoked) are sold both canned and dried.
They can be quite hot, so use one, or even just a half if you
enjoy a smoky flavor but do not care for heat.

10 sun-dried tomato halves
2 roasted red bell peppers, each cut in 3 to 4 pieces
    (see note)
2 large cloves garlic, coarsely chopped
1 to 2 canned chipotle chiles
1 (15-ounce) can Great Northern beans, rinsed and drained
5¼ ounces soft or firm silken tofu
1 teaspoon ground cumin
1 teaspoon dried oregano
¼ cup extra virgin olive oil
Salt

NOTE

For this dish, I recommend roasting the peppers
by baking them in the oven at 500 degrees until
they are slightly soft, about 15 minutes. Place the
peppers in a paper bag for 20 to 30 minutes, then
peel them. Use the roasted peppers at once or
refrigerate them in their juice. In the refrigerator,
they keep 2 to 3 days in a tightly sealed container.

1 In a small bowl, soak the tomatoes in just enough water to cover, until they are soft, about 30 minutes. Squeeze them to remove as much moisture as possible. Chop the tomatoes coarsely.

2 In a food processor, combine the tomatoes with the red peppers, garlic, and chipotle chile; process to a puree, about 2 minutes.

3 Add the beans and process until they are pureed into the tomato and pepper mixture.

4 Add the tofu, cumin, and oregano and process until well blended, 1 minute.

5 With the motor running, slowly add the olive oil in a thin stream through the feeder tube, blending it into the dip. Season to taste with salt. If not serving immediately, store the dip in a covered container and refrigerate; it keeps up to 2 days (beyond that, the garlic tends to taste bitter and the other flavors lose their freshness).

VARIATION

Omit the beans and use 10½ ounces of firm silken tofu (one package).

Aioli

YIELD: 1/2 CUP

In Provence, this classic, lusty accompaniment for bouilla-
baisse is made from raw garlic, egg yolks, and plenty of olive
oil. This version calls for roasted garlic, tofu, and a relatively
modest amount of fruity olive oil. Using roasted garlic adds
creamy texture. Replacing the eggs with bean curd removes
saturated fat. A good-quality extra virgin olive oil keeps
the lusty, sunny flavors of this aioli loud and clear. Serve
with crudités, dollop this aioli into soup, or enjoy it on
steamed vegetables.

2 ounces soft regular or silken tofu (about 1/4 cup)
2 heads garlic, roasted (about 1/4 cup)
2 teaspoons fresh lemon juice
Pinch of cayenne
1/4 teaspoon salt, or to taste
Freshly ground pepper
1/4 cup extra virgin olive oil

1 In a blender, puree the tofu with the garlic.
2 Add the lemon juice, cayenne, salt, and pepper and blend.
3 With the motor running, slowly add the olive oil in a thin, steady stream. Scrape the aioli into a small bowl. Cover tightly with plastic wrap and refrigerate for 1 hour, up to overnight, to allow the flavors to meld.

VARIATION

A cup of cooked white beans added with the tofu turns this into a thick spread. Throw in 2 to 3 more cloves of the roasted garlic along with the beans. Spread on grilled bread to make bruschetta.

MAIN DISHES

MAIN DISHES

*my favorite recipes

Sweet & Sour Tofu Stir-Fry

YIELD: 8 SERVINGS

Most sweet-and-sour dishes are cloyingly sweet. Fresh ingredients and light a sauce make this colorful stir-fry an exception. Full of crunch and contrasts, it is a dish you'll keep picking at even after you are full. Serve with brown rice or cooked millet.

2 cups broccoli florets
2 cups cauliflower florets
1 cup sliced carrots
1 tablespoon cornstarch
½ cup pineapple juice
1 tablespoon dark brown sugar
¼ cup apple juice concentrate
1 tablespoon rice vinegar
2 tablespoons peanut oil
1 tablespoon finely chopped peeled ginger root
2 cloves garlic, finely chopped
1 jalapeño pepper, seeded and cut lengthwise into thin strips

VARIATION

If you like Chinese Pepper Steak, here's a nice version: use 1½ cups each diced red and green bell peppers plus 1 cup sliced onions in place of the broccoli, cauliflower, and carrots. This combination is delicious with the tofu and sauce.

16 ounces firm or extra firm regular tofu, pan-crisped
   (see page 33)
1 large tomato, cut in 16 wedges
1 cup canned straw mushrooms, drained
⅓ cup preserved pineapple cut into ½-inch pieces (see note)
1 teaspoon salt
Freshly ground pepper

1 In a large pot of boiling water, cook the broccoli, cauliflower, and carrots for 3 minutes. With a slotted spoon, remove the vegetables from the pot and plunge immediately into ice water. Drain well and set the vegetables aside.

2 In a small bowl, combine the cornstarch and 2 tablespoons of the pineapple juice. In another small bowl, combine the brown sugar, apple juice concentrate, and the remaining pineapple juice with the rice vinegar. Set both bowls where you can reach them easily while stir-frying.

3 In a wok, heat the peanut oil. Add the ginger, garlic, and jalapeño. Stir-fry until the garlic and ginger are fragrant, about 1 minute. Add the drained vegetables and stir-fry 3 minutes.

NOTE

Fruit and nut shops use the terms "preserved" or "glazed" to describe this kind of candied pineapple, while natural food stores call it dried pineapple. You will recognize it as the kind you would cut up to use in fruitcake.

4 Add the tofu, tomato, mushrooms, and pineapple. Restir the fruit juice mixture to blend and add it while continuing to stir and toss the vegetables.

5 When all the ingredients in the wok are mixed together and the liquid is bubbling, restir the cornstarch mixture. Add this mixture to the wok, stirring constantly as the liquid thickens and clings to the vegetables. Season to taste with sale and pepper. Turn onto a platter and serve immediately, accompanied by rice. If there are leftovers, bring them to room temperature before serving rather than reheating them.

VARIATION

Substitute red bell pepper, cut in 1-inch pieces, for the tomatoes. This is a good choice when tomatoes in your market are like cardboard. If you like spicy food, use 1 or 2 green chile peppers in place of the milder jalapeños.

Sicilian Stuffed Squash

YIELD: 2 SERVINGS AS A MAIN DISH,
4 SERVINGS AS A LIGHT DISH

At Regaleali, the estate of the Tasca-Lanza family in Sicily, Monzù (chef) Mario LoMenzo stuffs swordfish involtini with a traditional filling of grated cheese, parsley, currants, bread crumbs, and herbs. Using TVP in place of the bread crumbs, this stuffing turns vegetables into a hearty main course. The saffron is also authentically Sicilian, since the Arabs brought this aromatic spice to the island along with pasta, citrus fruit, and sugarcane. Use a spoon rather than a melon-baller to remove the soft part of the squash, and there will be less risk of piercing through the bottom of the squash.

2 medium zucchini (each about ½ pound)
2 tablespoons extra virgin olive oil
½ cup finely chopped onion
⅓ cup TVP flakes
¼ teaspoon ground cinnamon
¾ teaspoon thyme leaves, or ¼ teaspoon dried thyme
1 large plum tomato, halved, seeded, and chopped
    (about ½ cup)
1 tablespoon tomato paste
6 saffron threads, soaked in 1 teaspoon warm water
    (optional)
3 tablespoons currants
2 tablespoons chopped Italian parsley
1½ tablespoons grated pecorino or
    soy Parmesan cheese
1 tablespoon dry bread crumbs
Salt and freshly ground pepper

1 Preheat the oven to 375 degrees.

2 Halve the squash lengthwise. To help the squash halves sit securely, cut a thin strip, ¾ inch by 4 inches, from the bottom of each one (this strip should be as thin as if you were peeling the squash). With a teaspoon, scoop out the flesh, making a long, narrow channel down the center of each squash half by removing only the soft, seeded part. Reserve enough of this scooped out flesh to make 1 cup, discarding the rest. Set aside the squash halves.

3 Prepare the filling: In a medium skillet, heat 1 tablespoon of the oil over medium-high heat. Sauté the onion until translucent, about 5 minutes. Mix in the reserved squash and cook 2 minutes, until it softens slightly, stirring occasionally. Add the TVP and cook, stirring, until it is coated with oil. Blend in the cinnamon and thyme. Stir in the tomato and cook 2 minutes, until it starts to soften. Blend in the tomato paste, saffron, if using, and ¼ cup water. Stir in the currants, parsley, and 1 tablespoon of the cheese. The filling will be moist and chunky. Season to taste with salt and pepper.

4 To fill the squash, place the four halves in a square baking dish or ovenproof serving dish just large enough to hold them. Pour ½ cup water into the bottom of the dish. Spoon a quarter of the filling into each of the squash halves, mounding it slightly. Leave the top end of the squash uncovered.

5 In a small bowl, mix the bread crumbs with the remaining cheese. Sprinkle this mixture evenly over each half, and drizzle the remaining olive oil over all.

6 Bake the squash, uncovered, in the middle of the oven for 45 minutes, until a knife inserted in the neck of the squash

easily pierces it. Remove the squash from the oven. Let stand
20 minutes and serve hot. Or let cool completely and serve the
squash at room temperature. If you plan to serve this dish
within 12 hours, cover the cooled squash with foil but do not
refrigerate; it will be more succulent and flavorful.

VARIATION

Substitute a cup of cooked rice for the bread
crumbs, then use the filling to stuff grape leaves.
Line a baking dish with orange slices, as Monzù
Mario does for his stuffed sardines, then arrange
the stuffed grape leaves in one layer over the or-
anges. Bake, covered, at 375 degrees for 30 minutes. Serve lukewarm.

Smokin' Black Soybean Chili with Corn

YIELD: 8 SERVINGS

Black soybeans have a slightly sweet flavor that gracefully rounds the dusky edge of the chipotle chilis in this fiery Southwestern dish. You'll find black soybeans at natural food stores, or you can order them by mail (see page 230)

2 chipotle chiles, dried or canned
2 tablespoons peanut oil
2 cups chopped onion
1 cup chopped green bell pepper
2 cloves garlic, minced
1 tablespoon ancho or New Mexico chile powder
1 tablespoon ground cumin
1 tablespoon dried oregano
1 tablespoon paprika
½ teaspoon ground cinnamon
¼ teaspoon cayenne

2 cups cooked black soybeans (see note)
1 (28-ounce) can plum tomatoes, chopped
¼ cup chopped fresh cilantro
1 bay leaf
1½ cups canned or frozen corn
Salt
Chopped cilantro, for garnish
Chopped onion, for garnish
Tofu Sour Cream (page 152)

1 If using dried chiles, in a small bowl, soak the peppers in ½ cup warm water until soft, about 30 minutes. Drain them, reserving the soaking liquid. Seed and chop the chiles. Set aside. If using canned peppers, simply drain and chop them.

2 In a 5-quart Dutch oven, heat the oil. Sauté the onion, green pepper, and garlic until the onion is translucent, about 8 minutes, stirring occasionally.

3 Mix in the chile powder, cumin, oregano, paprika, cinnamon, and cayenne until the vegetables are coated and the seasonings release their aroma, about 1 minute. Immediately add the soybeans, tomatoes, the chopped chiles with their soaking liquid, and 1 cup water. Mix in the ¼ cup cilantro and add the bay leaf. Simmer the chili 30 minutes.

4 Mix in the corn and cook until it is heated through. Add salt to taste and serve. Pass bowls containing cilantro, onion, and Tofu Sour Cream. Serve with brown rice, if desired.

NOTE

To cook black soybeans, soak 1 cup of the beans 8 hours, or overnight. Place in a medium pot with cold water. Bring to a boil. Reduce heat, cover, and simmer until cooked, about 2 hours.

VARIATION

Replace 1 cup of the soybeans with 1 cup each of chickpeas and navy beans. I like to serve this lighter version in summer, accompanied by corn chips.

Red Peppers Stuffed with Millet, Corn, and Tempeh

YIELD: 6 SERVINGS

My favorite stuffed peppers call for ingredients from Asia (millet and tempeh), the New World (corn and red bell peppers), and the Mediterranean (sun-dried tomatoes, oregano, and mint). Thin-walled, domestically-grown sweet peppers work better than the thickly fleshed, imported kind. This dish is an ideal choice for picnics and potlucks, since it travels well and tastes as good at room temperature as warm.

1½ cups Roasted Vegetable Stock (page 60), vegetable broth, or water
½ cup millet
6 medium red bell peppers
4 ounces (½ package) three-grain or other mild-flavored tempeh, coarsely chopped
¾ cup canned corn or defrosted frozen corn
¾ cup chopped onion
1 medium rib celery, chopped
8 marinated sun-dried tomato halves, lightly drained and chopped
2 cloves garlic, minced
1 teaspoon dried oregano
1 teaspoon dried mint
Salt and freshly ground pepper
2 tablespoons extra virgin olive oil
2 tablespoons fresh lemon juice

1 In a medium saucepan, bring the broth to a boil. Add the millet and return to a boil. Cover the pot, reduce the heat, and cook until the millet is soft, about 20 minutes. Remove from the heat and let the millet sit, covered, 5 minutes.

2 While the millet cooks, prepare the peppers: Remove the top from each pepper, cutting across horizontally far enough down so that the top can serve as a hat. Scoop out and discard the seeds and ribs from each pepper. If necessary, cut off just enough from the bottom of each pepper to make it stand firmly.

3 Preheat the oven to 375 degrees. Set a rack in the center of the oven. Select an ovenproof dish or shallow baking pan just large enough to hold the peppers.

4 Transfer the cooked millet to a mixing bowl. Add the tempeh, corn, onion, celery, tomatoes, garlic, oregano, and mint; mix to combine. Season to taste with salt and pepper. You will have about 3 cups of filling.

5 Scoop ½ cup of the filling into each pepper, packing until it mounds slightly. Brush the top of each stuffed pepper lightly with a bit of the olive oil. Arrange the peppers in the baking dish so that they almost touch one another.

6 Place the baking dish in the center of the oven. Pour ½ cup water into the bottom of the pan. Bake the peppers, uncovered, 45 minutes, until they are soft when pierced with the tip of a knife but still hold their shape.

7 In a small bowl, combine the remaining olive oil and the lemon juice. While the peppers are still warm, spoon about half a tablespoon of this mixture over each one. Serve the peppers warm or at room temperature.

VARIATION

This filling works nicely on its own as a grain dish. Simply pack it into a lightly oiled ovenproof dish, cover with foil, and bake at 375 degrees for 40 minutes. Serve with steamed greens.

Choucroute Garnie

YIELD: 4 SERVINGS

It's been years since I dug into the heroic Choucroute Garnie at Brasserie Lipp in Paris. In fact, today I probably could not make a dent in this gargantuan heap of meats, sausage, and champagne-doused sauerkraut. These days, pan-seared tempeh braised in sauerkraut served at The Kripalu Center, a yoga community in Lenox, Massachusetts, is more my style. Combining aspects of both dishes, this recipe marries tempeh, lightly blackened in a dry pan as they do at Kripalu, with the tang of sauerkraut cooked with white wine, and caraway. When squeezing out the sauerkraut, leave a bit of moisture so it does not go limp.

1 (8-ounce) package soy or quinoa and millet tempeh
½ cup dry white wine
¼ cup natural soy sauce
2 large cloves garlic, halved lengthwise
1 (1-inch) piece ginger root, peeled and thinly sliced
½ cup vegetable broth
½ teaspoon black peppercorns
2 medium white or yellow potatoes
1 (32-ounce) jar natural sauerkraut
½ teaspoon caraway seeds

1 Prepare the tempeh: Cut it crosswise into 2 pieces and halve each piece horizontally. Leaving the 2 layers stacked, cut each piece of tempeh into 4 squares, making 8 pieces. Cut the stacked pieces in half diagonally, making 16 triangles. Repeat with the second block of tempeh, making 32 triangles in all. In a large glass baking dish or nonreactive pan, arrange the 32 pieces of tempeh in one layer. Set aside.

2 In a small, nonreactive saucepan, combine ¼ cup of the wine, the soy sauce, garlic, ginger, broth, and peppercorns and bring to a boil. Reduce the heat and simmer until this mixture is reduced by one-fourth, 3 to 4 minutes. Pour the hot marinade over the tempeh and let it sit until the liquid has cooled to room temperature. Cover the dish and marinate the tempeh in the refrigerator for 8 to 24 hours.

3 Bring a pot of water large enough to hold the potatoes to a boil. Add the potatoes, and cook until they are almost done when pierced with a thin knife.

4 Meanwhile, drain the sauerkraut in a colander. A handful at a time, squeeze most of the remaining liquid from the sauerkraut, leaving it just lightly moist. You will have about 2 cups of drained sauerkraut when you are done. (You can do this stage ahead and refrigerate the sauerkraut in a covered container.)

5 Drain the tempeh, reserving ¼ cup of the marinade and discarding the rest. With paper towels, blot the tempeh dry.

6 Place a large, heavy skillet over medium-high heat. Add the triangles of tempeh to the hot, dry skillet and cook, pressing on the tempeh gently with a spatula, until the pieces are lightly charred, 2 to 3 minutes. Turn and char the other side. Remove the tempeh from the skillet and set aside. Repeat with the remaining tempeh.

7 In the same pan used for the tempeh, combine the reserved marinade, the remaining wine, the sauerkraut, and caraway seeds. Simmer over medium heat until the liquid is reduced by half, stirring occasionally.

8 Add the tempeh, combining it gently with the sauerkraut so the pieces do not crumble. Cook until the tempeh is hot, about 10 minutes.

9 Meanwhile, when the potatoes are cool enough to handle, peel and cut them into 8 pieces. Add the potatoes to the sauerkraut and tempeh. Remove the pan from the heat and serve. This dish is also good served lukewarm.

VARIATION

For a Tempeh Reuben Sandwich, cut the tempeh into 4 squares. Marinate and char as above. Place one piece of tempeh on a slice of whole wheat bread. Top it with ¼ cup drained sauerkraut and a slice of Swiss cheese. Spread a second slice of bread liberally with Real Russian Dressing (page 167) and place it, dressing-side down, over the cheese. Coat a skillet with nonstick spray. When the pan is hot, grill the sandwich until the cheese melts and the bread is toasted on both sides.

Wild Mushroom and Tofu Ragout

YIELD: 12 SERVINGS

Here is a great dish for holiday feasting. The cubes of tofu take on the same appealing mahogany color as the lusty sauce. The chunks of mushroom add meaty texture. Urbani's Second-Choice dried porcini mushrooms plump up to a silky texture and contribute deep, concentrated flavor while letting you keep the cost of this dish well in hand. Doubling the recipe is easy when you need to feed a large group.

2 ounces dried porcini mushrooms
¼ cup olive oil
1½ cups chopped leek, white and pale green parts
16 ounces white mushrooms, stemmed and very thinly sliced
2 pounds cremini mushrooms, stemmed and cut in
      1-inch cubes
2½ pounds portobello mushrooms, stemmed and cut in
      1-inch cubes, or 2 (6-ounce) packages sliced portobellos,
      cut crosswise into 1-inch pieces
1 cup dry red wine
6 cloves garlic, roasted
2 teaspoons finely chopped rosemary, or 1 teaspoon
      dried rosemary
16 onces firm or extra firm regular tofu, pressed and
      cut in ¾-inch cubes
1 bay leaf
Salt and freshly ground pepper
Chopped Italian parsley

1 In a medium bowl, cover the dried porcini with enough warm (not hot) water to cover. Soak the mushrooms until soft, 20 to 40 minutes. Lift them from their soaking liquid. Squeeze as much moisture as possible from the mushrooms, holding them over the bowl containing their soaking water as you work, to capture the intensely flavored liquid being pressed out. Reserve all the liquid. Chop the mushrooms; you should have about 1½ cups.

2 In a large Dutch oven or heavy pot, heat the oil over medium-high heat. Add the leek and cook until it softens, about 6 minutes, stirring occasionally.

3 Stir in the white mushrooms and cook until they give up their liquid, 6 to 8 minutes. Add the chopped porcini mushrooms. Reduce the heat to medium and cook until the mushrooms are meltingly soft, about 15 minutes, stirring occasionally. Stir in the cremini and portobello mushrooms. Return the heat to medium-high and cook until the additional mushrooms give up their liquid, about 10 minutes, stirring occasionally. Cook the mushrooms, stirring often, until most of the liquid has boiled away, 5 to 7 minutes. Some of the mixture will stick to the pot; scrape up as much as possible, taking care not to let it burn.

4 Add the red wine and simmer vigorously until it has almost evaporated, about 5 minutes.

5 Squeeze the roasted garlic from its peel and blend it into the mushrooms, along with the rosemary. Stir in 1 cup of the reserved mushroom soaking liquid. Add the tofu and bay leaf. Reduce the heat to medium and simmer the ragout until the portobello mushrooms are tender yet firm to the bite. Add more of the mushroom soaking liquid, if necessary, to keep the mixture just moist. Remove the bay leaf. Season to taste with salt and pepper. To serve, ladle the ragout into a tureen and garnish with the parsley. Or let the ragout cool and store it, tightly covered, for up to 3 days. Reheat in a covered pot in a 350-degree oven for 20 minutes.

VARIATION

When you add the garlic, also stir in a cup of cooked chestnuts. They add a lovely flavor and make this dish even more festive.

Unstuffed Cabbage

YIELD: 8 SERVINGS

When I am under the weather, all I want to eat is large bowls of steaming "Medestrone" with Cabbage and Sauerkraut, a stew-like soup from Maggie Waldron's *Cold Spaghetti at Midnight*. This dense soup contains most of the ingredients used in making stuffed cabbage. Having watched my grandmother and mother laboriously assemble batches of stuffed cabbage, I decided to combine the deliciously tart-sweet tang of their recipe and TVP to the Medestrone, transforming this meatless dish into a one-pot meal, loaded with warm family memories and restorative goodness.

2 tablespoons olive oil

1 large onion, chopped

2 cloves garlic, chopped

¾ cup TVP flakes

1 pound cabbage (about half a medium head), quartered, cored, and cut crosswise into ½-inch strips

4 carrots, chopped

2 ribs celery, chopped

1 (28-ounce) can plum tomatoes, drained and chopped

1 turnip, peeled and quartered

½ teaspoon black peppercorns

4 cups Roasted Vegetable Stock (page 60) or water

1 (16-ounce) can sauerkraut, rinsed and squeezed dry

3 tablespoons fresh lemon juice

1 to 3 tablespoons honey or unbleached cane sugar, according to taste

1 bay leaf

Salt and freshly ground pepper

½ cup minced dill

½ cup minced Italian parsley

Sour cream (soy or cow's milk) (optional)

1 In a large pot or Dutch oven, heat the oil over medium-high heat. Sauté the onion and garlic until the onion is lightly browned, 10 to 12 minutes.

2 Mix in the TVP, stirring until it has darkened from absorbing some of the oil in the vegetables.

3 Add the cabbage, carrots, celery, tomatoes, turnip, and peppercorns. Pour in the stock and bring to a boil. Reduce the heat and simmer 1 hour.

4 Add the sauerkraut, lemon juice, honey, and bay leaf. Simmer 1 hour more, adding water if necessary.

5 Remove the bay leaf and season to taste with salt and pepper. Ladle into bowls. Garnish each bowl with a tablespoon each of the dill and parsley and serve, accompanied by the sour cream, if using.

VARIATION

In place of the TVP, sometimes I use 1 pound of firm regular tofu cut into 1-inch cubes. The tofu is added along with the cabbage and tomatoes.

Lentil Lasagna

YIELD: 10 SERVINGS

Lentils are remarkably versatile, as you see in this lasagna. The sunny Mediterranean warmth of red wine and spices in this dish are a perfect complement to the creamy tofu topping. For the pasta, I prefer semolina or Jerusalem artichoke ribbons, but whole wheat or spelt lasagna noodles are fine too. This lasagna freezes well, so while you are at it, why not double the recipe and store the spare portion.

2 tablespoons extra virgin olive oil
2/3 cup finely chopped carrot
1½ cups finely chopped onion
2 cloves garlic, minced
2 cups green lentils
3 cups Roasted Vegetable Stock (page 60), vegetable broth, or water
¾ teaspoon ground cinnamon
½ teaspoon dried oregano
½ teaspoon dried basil
2 tablespoons tomato paste
1 (28-ounce) can plum tomatoes, drained
1 cup dry red wine
1 to 2 bay leaves
9 lasagna noodles
8 ounces soft regular tofu
6 tablespoons grated cow's milk or soy Parmesan cheese
2 teaspoons fresh lemon juice
Salt and freshly ground pepper

1 Prepare the lentil filling: In a large saucepan, heat the oil. Add the carrots, onions, and garlic; cook until the vegetables soften, 10 minutes. Add the lentils and 2 cups of the stock;

bring to a boil, reduce the heat, cover, and simmer until the lentils are al dente, about 30 minutes.

2 Stir in the cinnamon, oregano, basil, and tomato paste. Add the tomatoes, crushing them with the back of a wooden spoon. Stir in the wine and bay leaf. Cook, adding the remaining stock to the lentils ½ cup at a time as needed, until the lentils are soft, about 30 minutes. Remove the bay leaf. Season to taste with salt and pepper. (This part of the lasagna may be prepared 2 to 3 days ahead.)

3 In a large pot of boiling water, cook the lasagna noodles according to package directions. Drain well.

4 To assemble the lasagna, cover the bottom of a 13 by 2 by 9-inch ovenproof dish with 3 lasagna noodles. Top the noodles with half the lentil mixture, smoothing it to make an even layer. Cover with 3 more of the lasagna noodles. Top with the remaining lentil mixture. Finish with the remaining lasagna noodles.

5 Prepare the topping: In a food processor or blender, puree the tofu with 4 tablespoons of the cheese and the lemon juice. With a rubber spatula, spread this mixture over the lasagna. (The lasagna can be made ahead up to this point, covered tightly with foil, and refrigerated or frozen.)

6 Preheat the oven to 375 degrees. Sprinkle the remaining 2 tablespoons of Parmesan cheese over the lasagna. Bake until the lasagna is heated through, about 45 minutes. To reheat frozen lasagna, cover it with foil and bake 30 minutes. Uncover and continue cooking until it is hot.

VARIATION

If you make a double batch of the lentil filling, turn the extra portion into a casserole. Add sautéed mushrooms, cooked spinach, and cooked brown rice. Bake, covered, at 350 degrees until heated through.

Mushroom Chili

YIELD: 6 SERVINGS

Meaty mushrooms and TVP are the base for this mild "bowl of red." It is a classic chili, accented by the floral notes of jalapeños. This is a great way to discover the virtues of TVP.

2 tablespoons olive oil

1 cup chopped onion

3 to 6 cloves garlic, chopped, according to taste

1½ cups chopped green bell pepper

2 large jalapeño peppers, seeded and minced

1 tablespoon chili powder

1 teaspoon ground cumin

1 teaspoon dried oregano

1 (10-ounce) package white mushrooms, stemmed
    and quartered

½ pound cremini mushrooms, stemmed and quartered

1 cup TVP flakes

6 large plum tomatoes, halved, seeded, and chopped
    (about 2 cups)

2 cups Roasted Vegetable Stock (page 60) or water

2 tablespoons meaty miso, such as red, aka, or hatcho

Salt and freshly ground pepper

1 In a small Dutch oven, heat the oil over medium-high heat. Sauté the onion, garlic, green pepper, and jalapeños until the onion softens, about 5 minutes, stirring often. Mix in the chili powder, cumin, and oregano and cook, stirring, until the spices release their aroma, about 1 minute. Take care not to let them burn.

2 Add the mushrooms and cook until they start to give up their liquid, about 5 minutes, stirring occasionally. Mix in the TVP, stirring until it absorbs some of the moisture from the vegetables, about 2 minutes. Mix in the tomatoes and cook just until they soften slightly, about 3 minutes.

3 Pour in the stock and bring the chili to a boil. Reduce the heat and simmer, uncovered, 15 minutes. The chili will be soupy but not swimming in liquid.

4 Place the miso in a cup or small bowl. Add 2 tablespoons of liquid from the chili. Cream the miso until it is well blended with the liquid. Remove the pot of chili from the heat, and mix the miso into the chili. Season to taste with salt and pepper. Serve over cooked rice.

VARIATIONS

••

Try 2 cups cooked lentils in place of the TVP. Or use 1 cup TVP and 1 cup lentils.

For a fiery version of this chili, substitute a habeñero chile for the jalapeños.

Tofu in Coriander–Mustard Sauce with Kohlrabi and Pears

YIELD: 6 SERVINGS

This was the most popular main dish I offered when I ran a catering service during the early '80s. In those days, I made it with chicken. As requests for meatless meals increased, I found that tofu worked even better than the poultry because of the way it took up the aromatic, golden sauce. This festive stew keeps 2 to 3 days and reheats well, making it perfect for parties. Serve it over rice accompanied by a green salad and baby carrots braised in orange juice.

2 tablespoons canola oil
1 cup finely chopped onion
2 tablespoons finely minced shallots
2 heaping tablespoons flour
1 cup hard cider or apple juice (see note)
½ cup Dijon mustard
1 tablespoon ground coriander
16 ounces firm regular tofu, pressed, cut in ¾-inch cubes
1 medium kohlrabi, peeled, cut in ¾-inch cubes
1 Bosc pear, peeled and cored, cut in ¾-inch pieces
8 ounces mushrooms, stemmed and quartered
Salt and freshly ground pepper

1 In a Dutch oven, heat the oil over medium-high heat. Add the onion and shallots. Cook until the onion is soft, about 5 minutes, stirring occasionally. Stir in the flour, mixing to coat the onion. Cook 3 minutes, stirring constantly, so the flour does not color.

2 Using a wooden spoon, stir in ¼ cup of the cider. Scrape the pot with the wooden spoon to gather up and dissolve any flour that sticks to the bottom and sides of the pan. As soon as the mixture thickens, add the remaining cider, stirring until you have a thick sauce.

3 Mix the mustard and coriander into the sauce. Add the tofu and kohlrabi. Simmer gently for 15 minutes.

4 Add the pear and mushrooms and simmer until the pear pieces are tender, 10 to 15 minutes. Season to taste with salt and pepper. Serve over rice.

NOTE

Hard cider imported from France can be found in liquor stores. It is drier in flavor than apple juice and only mildly alcoholic. What you don't pour into the pot is delicious served chilled along with this dish.

VARIATION

Use ½ cup chopped leeks in place of the shallots and a diced Golden Delicious apple in place of the pear. This makes a more casual, heartier version of this off-beat stew.

Indonesian Coconut Apple Curry

YIELD: 6 SERVINGS

When I was a teenager, long before the trend of authentic Asian cooking took hold, dining on the Indian curry at the Pierre Grill in New York felt like the height of sophistication. This was a mild, creamy dish in the English or French style. Best of all, a waiter presented a tray of garnishes to choose from, including grated coconut, raisins, chopped roasted peanuts, and Major Grey's chutney. This Indonesian-style curry includes most of these ingredients right in the curry. Major Grey's fruity chutney would still be the perfect accompaniment.

2 tablespoons canola oil
1 cup finely chopped onion
2 tablespoons finely chopped shallots
1 Golden Delicious apple, peeled, cored, and chopped
1 teaspoon ground ginger
1 teaspoon ground coriander
½ teaspoon ground cumin
½ teaspoon ground turmeric
¼ teaspoon ground cardamom
⅛ teaspoon ground cinnamon
½ cup grated fresh coconut or dried, unsweetened coconut
    (see note)

NOTE

Natural food stores and Asian markets sell dried, unsweetened coconut.

1 cup Roasted Vegetable Stock (page 60), vegetable
     broth, or water
16 ounces firm or extra firm tofu, pressed and cut in
     1-inch cubes
1 medium green bell pepper, diced
3 scallions, white and green parts, cut in ½-inch slices
⅓ cup chopped roasted peanuts

1 In a wok or large, heavy skillet, heat the oil over high heat.
  Add the onion and stir-fry or sauté until it has softened, 3 to
  4 minutes. Add the shallots and apple and stir-fry 1 minute
  more.
2 Quickly add the ginger, coriander, cumin, turmeric, cardamom, and cinnamon. Stir to blend the spices with the onions
  and apple. Mix in the coconut. Stir in the stock. Reduce the
  heat and simmer for 3 minutes.
3 Add the tofu, green pepper, and scallions. Simmer until the
  curry has thickened slightly and the tofu is heated through; the
  pepper and scallions should be crisp-tender. Transfer the curry
  to a serving dish. Garnish with the chopped nuts and serve
  immediately, accompanied by boiled rice.

VARIATION

Brown 8 ounces of cubed tempeh and use it in
place of the tofu. In this version, I often use a sweet
red pepper instead of the green one.

Red Curried Tofu

YIELD: 6 SERVINGS

Tofu, with its affinity for intensely flavored sauces, is perfect in this curry exploding with Thai spices. Most Thai cooks buy their curry paste ready-made, assures Nancie McDermott, author of *Real Thai*. I recommend any of the Thai curry pastes now sold at natural food stores, conventional supermarkets, and Asian food markets. These stores also carry coconut milk, another key ingredient in Thai curry. (I prefer Thai Kitchen brand, because it does not contain sodium bisulfite.) If you hesitate to use fish sauce because you are vegetarian, Nancy, who lived in Thailand, says that even devout Buddhists consider it integral to good cooking and use it without qualms. But you can substitute soy sauce and fresh lime juice, if you prefer.

8 to 10 large fresh basil leaves
½ cup canned coconut milk
2 tablespoons red Thai curry paste
1 tablespoon fish sauce (optional)
1 tablespoon unbleached cane sugar
1 cup butternut, kabocha, or other hard winter squash,
    peeled and cut in ½-inch pieces
1 cup green beans, cut in 1-inch pieces
1 medium red bell pepper, cut in ½-inch strips
16 ounces extra firm regular tofu, pressed if desired, cut in
    ½-inch cubes

1 Stack the basil leaves. Roll them lengthwise. Cut crosswise into ¼-inch shreds and set aside.

2 In a wok or large, heavy skillet over medium-high heat, heat the coconut milk until the surface glistens with oil. Blend in the curry paste until it dissolves. Mix in the fish sauce, if using, and the sugar.

3 Mix the squash, beans, and red pepper into the sauce. Add the tofu. Reduce the heat and simmer until the vegetables are crisp-tender, about 5 minutes. Mix in the shredded basil. Serve the curry immediately, accompanied by cooked aromatic rice such as jasmine or basmati.

VARIATION

Use green bell pepper, zucchini, and cooked potatoes in place of the winter squash, green beans, and red bell pepper. Add the pepper and zucchini at the time you would the squash and beans. Add the potatoes near the end, in place of the red pepper.

Gado Gado with Stir-Fry Vegetables

YIELD: 4 SERVINGS

Gado Gado—steamed vegetables topped with creamy peanut sauce—is a common dish in Indonesia. It is a great way to enjoy vegetables. For this version, the vegetables are stir-fried instead of steamed. Miso adds rich notes to the peanut sauce. Serve on a bed of cooked brown rice or millet, if you wish.

3 large dried shiitake mushrooms
½ cup unsweetened smooth peanut butter
2 large cloves garlic, minced
2 tablespoons natural soy sauce
1 tablespoon plus 1 teaspoon maple syrup
1 tablespoon plus 1 teaspoon roasted sesame oil
2 teaspoons shiro miso (see note)
2 teaspoons rice vinegar
Pinch of cayenne, or to taste
3 tablespoons cold-pressed sesame oil or peanut oil
½ red bell pepper, seeded, cut in 2 by ¼-inch strips
1 medium carrot, cut in 2 by ¼-inch sticks
2 cups napa cabbage, cut in ½-inch slices
2 cups bean sprouts
1 scallion, white and green parts, cut in 2-inch lengths
¼ cup minced fresh coriander

NOTE

"Shiro" means white. This pale miso is sold at both natural and Japanese food stores.

1 In a small bowl, pour ⅔ cup warm water over the mushrooms. Soak until they are soft, 25 to 30 minutes. Remove the mushrooms, squeezing them gently over the bowl to extract any excess liquid. Reserve the soaking liquid. Cut away and discard the mushroom stems. Stack the mushrooms and slice them into ¼-inch strips. Set aside.

2 Prepare the sauce: In a food processor or blender, combine the peanut butter, garlic, soy sauce, maple syrup, roasted sesame oil, miso, rice vinegar, and cayenne. Add ½ cup of the mushroom soaking liquid; process to blend. Set the sauce aside.

3 Prepare the vegetables: In a wok, heat the oil over high heat. Add the red pepper and carrot; stir-fry 2 to 3 minutes. Add the cabbage and sliced mushrooms; stir-fry 1 minute. Add the bean sprouts and scallion; stir-fry 30 seconds. Quickly transfer the vegetables to a platter or large bowl. Top with the sauce. Garnish with the cilantro and serve, accompanied by brown rice or millet.

VARIATION

Stir-fry cubes of tempeh or regular tofu along with the vegetables. Tempeh would be more authentic, of course. However, it's best when browned in peanut oil, while the tofu can simply be added as is.

Groundnut Stew

YIELD: 6 SERVINGS

In Africa, peanuts are known as groundnuts. They are used in many West African dishes. Traditionally, West African groundnut stew recipes call for beef. However, tofu replaces it nicely in this mildly hot, creamy dish. Use smooth peanut butter or your stew will have a gritty texture. Green beans and potatoes go nicely with this stew.

1 tablespoon peanut oil
1 cup chopped onion
1½ cups chopped green bell pepper
2 cloves garlic, minced
1 (½-inch) piece ginger root, peeled and chopped
½ cup smooth peanut butter
4 to 5 canned plum tomatoes, coarsely chopped, with
     enough of their liquid to make 1 cup
1 teaspoon unbleached cane sugar or dried sugarcane juice
½ teaspoon ground cinnamon
½ teaspoon dried thyme
¼ teaspoon ground allspice
Pinch to ½ teaspoon dried hot pepper flakes
1 cup Roasted Vegetable Stock (page 60) or water
1½ tablespoons fresh lemon juice
16 ounces firm regular tofu, pressed, cut in 1-inch cubes
Salt and freshly ground pepper

1 In a medium skillet with a cover, heat the oil. Sauté the onion and green pepper until the onion is translucent, about 5 minutes, stirring occasionally. Add the garlic and ginger and cook 2 minutes longer. Mix in the peanut butter, tomatoes, sugar, cinnamon, thyme, allspice, and pepper flakes. Stir in the stock and mix until all the ingredients are well blended and the peanut butter is completely dissolved. Blend in the lemon juice.

2 Mix the tofu into the peanut mixture. Bring to a boil, reduce the heat, and simmer the stew until the sauce is thick, about 15 minutes, stirring occasionally to prevent sticking. Serve accompanied by cooked rice. This dish keeps 2 to 3 days in the refrigerator. Adjust the seasoning after reheating.

VARIATION

Use pan-crisped tofu (page 33) and replace half the vegetable stock with ½ cup of tomato juice. The sauce will have a rosy color and the final dish a milder peanut flavor with a tomato tang.

Tofu "Scallops" Ritz Carlton

YIELD: 4 SERVINGS

Gary Danko created this stunning *trompe l'oeil* dish while he was chef at the dining room of the Ritz-Carlton Hotel in San Francisco. Although making it requires a number of steps, each is easy, and much of the work can be done ahead, as noted. If you can get someone to work with you in the kitchen, arrange each serving on the plate as they do at the Ritz. The beauty of this presentation makes the extra effort worthwhile.

Red Pepper Sauce
1 roasted red bell pepper, peeled and seeded
2 cloves garlic, smashed
1 tablespoon soy sauce
¼ teaspoon chopped ginger root
½ teaspoon roasted sesame oil
Salt and freshly ground pepper

Vegetables
1 roasted red bell pepper, peeled and seeded
8 small fresh shiitake mushrooms
5 tablespoons canola oil
1 Japanese eggplant cut diagonally into 12 slices,
    each ½-inch thick
Salt and freshly ground pepper

Tofu and Marinade

16 ounces extra firm regular tofu

1 cup soy sauce

¼ cup dry sherry

4 cloves garlic, chopped

2 tablespoons minced ginger root

¼ cup roasted sesame oil

12 asparagus tips, steamed and cooled in ice water

12 cauliflower florets, steamed and cooled in ice water

4 teaspoons pickled sushi ginger (optional)

1 tablespoon sesame seeds

1 Prepare the sauce: Coarsely chop the red pepper. Place it in a blender, along with the garlic, soy sauce, ginger, and sesame oil, and puree. Blend in 2½ tablespoons water. Season to taste with salt and pepper. Set aside. (This sauce can be prepared up to 8 hours ahead. Refrigerate in a tightly covered container. Bring to room temperature before using.)

2 Prepare the vegetables: Cut the red pepper open to make one long, flat strip. Using a biscuit cutter or round cookie cutter, punch out 4 rounds from the pepper. Set them aside on a large plate. Reserve the remaining pepper for another use. Brush the mushrooms lightly with some of the oil. In a skillet over medium-high heat, sauté the mushrooms until they are tender. Set aside with the red pepper rounds. Brush the eggplant slices with 2 tablespoons of the oil, coating both sides. Season lightly with salt and pepper. Arrange the eggplant on a baking sheet in 1 layer. Bake until the eggplant is just tender. Transfer to a plate.

3 Prepare the tofu: Cover a baking sheet with a double layer of paper towels. Slice the tofu horizontally in half. Arrange the tofu in one layer on the toweling. Cover with a double layer of paper towels. Top with another baking sheet and weight lightly. (Two cookbooks work nicely.) Let the tofu sit 10 minutes, just to remove excess water, not to press the tofu into a firmer texture. Unwrap the tofu and place it on a clean cutting board. Using a 1½-inch round cookie cutter, cut out "scallops" from the pressed tofu. If you do not have a cookie cutter, cut the tofu into 1-inch cubes.

4 About 30 minutes before serving, preheat the oven to 400 degrees.

5 In a bowl, whisk together the soy sauce, sherry, garlic, ginger, and sesame oil. Pour half the marinade into a rectangular nonreactive dish, large enough to hold the scallops in one layer. Add the "scallops." They may just touch, but do not squeeze them in or they will not absorb the marinade. Pour the remaining marinade over the tofu and let sit for just 10 minutes. Lift the "scallops" from the marinade and pat dry with a paper towel, reserving the marinade. Do not overmarinate the tofu. If it sits longer than 10 minutes, the intense taste of the marinade will throw the rest of the flavors of the dish out of balance.

6 While the tofu marinates, heat the vegetables. Arrange the red pepper and eggplant on a lightly oiled baking sheet and reheat in the oven. Meanwhile, in a large nonstick skillet, heat 1 tablespoon of the canola oil. Add the mushrooms, asparagus, and cauliflower, along with 2 tablespoons water to help the vegetables heat without coloring. When the vegetables are heated through, set them aside, covered to keep them warm.

7 To cook the tofu, wipe out the pan from the vegetables with a paper towel. Replace the pan over medium-high heat. Add the remaining oil and heat. Add the tofu and sauté just until the edges are lightly browned, about 2 minutes. Turn the tofu, and brown the other side. Transfer the tofu to a warm plate.

8 Pour the reserved marinade into the hot pan and bring it to a boil. Remove the pan from the heat and set aside.

9 Set out 4 warmed dinner plates. Drizzle each plate with 3 tablespoons of the red pepper sauce. Arrange 3 of the tofu "scallops" in the center of the plate. To one side, arrange 3 of the eggplant slices to make a fan. On the other side, arrange 1 disk of red pepper, 1 mushroom, 3 asparagus tips, and 3 cauliflower florets. Spoon a tablespoon of the warm marinade over the tofu. Arrange a mound of sushi ginger at the base of the eggplant slices, if using this garnish. Sprinkle sesame seeds over the plate. Repeat, making 4 servings. For a less formal presentation, use a large serving platter. Pour the red pepper sauce to fill the center of the platter. Set the "scallops" over the sauce. Arrange the vegetables around the tofu and serve.

VARIATION

Marinate the tofu, sauté it, and serve it on a bed of stir-fried eggplant, carrots, baby bok choy, and shiitake mushrooms.

PASTA AND
LIGHT DISHES

PASTA AND LIGHT DISHES

*my favorite recipes

Creamy Basil Cheesecake

YIELD: 10 SERVINGS

You'll find the same seductive pleasure in this savory treat as in The Creamiest Tofu Cheesecake in the World (page 194). In this recipe, I recommend using authentic Parmigiano-Reggiano cheese over soy Parmesan, unless you do not eat animal-based dairy. Thick slices of summer-ripe tomato are the perfect accompaniment to this dish.

Dairy-Free Pie Crust dough (page 184)
16 ounces soft silken tofu
16 ounces tofu cream cheese
2 eggs
⅔ cup grated cow's milk or soy Parmesan cheese
¼ cup onion, finely minced
1 cup finely shredded fresh basil, loosely packed
1 tablespoon fresh lemon juice
Generous pinch cayenne
1 teaspoon salt
3 tablespoons arrowroot powder

1 For the crust: Roll one-third of the dough out in a circle to fit the bottom of a 7-inch springform pan, making the dough as thin as possible. Place the dough over the bottom and trim it to fit. Snap the crust-covered pan bottom into place inside the collar of the pan.

2 Roll out a strip of dough long enough to line the sides of the pan. Make the dough wide enough to overlap the bottom by ½ inch and reach to ¾ inch below the top of the pan. This will take about half the remaining crust. Ease the dough into place. If it tears, press it together against the sides of the pan. Trim the top into a straight line ¾ inch below the top of the pan. Refrigerate the crust until the filling is prepared. (Cover the pan with plastic, and it can be held up to 24 hours before filling.)

3 Preheat the oven to 350 degrees. Set a rack in the center of the oven.

4 Prepare the filling: In a food processor, puree the tofu. Add the cheese and blend until combined with the tofu. It may be necessary to stop the motor and scrape down the sides of the bowl 2 or 3 times. Blend in the eggs.

NOTE

Refrigerating makes this cake more dense. To enjoy it at its creamiest, serve it the day it is made.

5 Add the Parmesan cheese, onion, and basil, and process to blend, scraping down the sides as needed. Add the lemon juice, cayenne, and salt and pepper, processing just until they are blended in. Mix in the arrowroot powder just until combined. Pour the filling into the prepared pan.

6 Bake the cheesecake in the center of the oven 50 to 60 minutes. The cake will be lightly browned on top. It should jiggle in the center. Turn off the heat but leave the cake in the oven for 60 minutes. The top of the cake will be browned and just soft to the touch in the center. Set the cake on a rack to cool at room temperature. Release the cake from the pan and serve, or refrigerate in the pan overnight, then bring back to room temperature and serve.

VARIATIONS

Use the dough to line miniature tart pans or the cavities of a miniature muffin tin. Fill almost to the top with the basil mixture. Bake at 350 degrees until the filling is set and the crust is lightly colored, about 20 minutes. Serve warm as an hors d'oeuvre. These miniature tarts can be prepared ahead, then reheated, but the filling will be more moist and dense, rather like quiche.

You can also use this filling to make a variation on Greek spanokopita: Prepare the phyllo according to the package directions and use this mixture in place of one made with spinach.

Spinach and Noodle Pudding

YIELD: 8 SERVINGS

Jewish cooks call this sweet and savory pudding a kugel. Traditionally, it is served as a side dish or as part of a light meal. Barney Stein, a caterer and brilliantly intuitive cook, created this soy version. Pecorino Romano is a sharp and salty Italian cheese made from sheep's milk. If you are vegan, soy Parmesan cheese, although milder, works nicely. I use Spectrum Spread because it adds buttery flavor; canola oil can be used in its place.

2 pounds fresh spinach, stemmed and chopped, or
    2 (10-ounce) packages frozen spinach, defrosted
4 ounces eggless noodles
2 (10-ounce) packages soft or firm silken tofu, or
    1 (16-ounce) tub firm regular tofu, drained
½ cup grated Pecorino Romano cheese
    or soy Parmesan cheese
2 teaspoons Spectrum Spread or canola oil
½ cup finely chopped onion
¼ cup dried currants
1 tablespoon grated lemon zest
½ teaspoon freshly ground pepper
Salt

1 Preheat the oven to 350 degrees. Set a rack in the center of the oven. Generously grease an 8-cup loaf pan with nonstick cooking spray.

2 If using fresh spinach, cook until it is just wilted, 2 to 3 minutes. If using frozen spinach, cook until it is defrosted and loses its raw taste, about 5 minutes. Drain the spinach in a colander. Run cold water over it to stop the cooking. Squeeze as much moisture as possible from the spinach, a handful at a time. Set aside.

3 Meanwhile, cook the noodles according to the package directions, leaving them slightly al dente. Drain well and set aside.

4 In a food processor, pulse the tofu until coarsely chopped. Add the cheese and pulse to blend. Set aside.

5 Using a paper towel, coat a cold medium skillet with Spectrum Spread. Add the onion to the cold pan and stir until the onion is coated. Place the pan over low heat, and cook until the spread melts. Increase the heat to medium-high and cook until the onion is very soft, about 6 minutes, stirring frequently. Take care the onion does not color.

6 Add the drained spinach to the pan and stir until it is blended with the onion and heated through. Remove from the heat.

7 Stir the tofu and cheese mixture into the spinach, blending well. Mix in the noodles, currants, lemon zest, and pepper. Season to taste with salt.

8 Pack the mixture into the prepared pan. Bake it in the center of the oven until a knife inserted in the center of the pudding comes out clean and the edges are lightly browned, 45 to 55 minutes. Run a sharp knife around the sides of the pan, then let the pudding rest 20 minutes before unmolding. With a sharp knife, cut the pudding into thick slices and serve, hot or lukewarm. Any leftovers should be reheated only to lukewarm.

VARIATIONS

In place of the noodles, use 2 cups cooked rice or millet. If you like a sweet pudding, blend ¼ cup unbleached sugar into the tofu and cheese mixture.

Red Flannel Hash

YIELD: 4 SERVINGS

If you have a leftover Yukon Gold, Yellow Finn, or other
golden potato on hand plus a can of beets, this is an easy
dish to put together. Tempeh bacon is what makes the
recipe work; its smoky flavor is perfect in place of corned
beef. Serve the hash with an egg on top and accompanied
by hash browns, as they do at the local diner, or enjoy it
as a light supper with a green salad on the side. And remember to pass the ketchup.

1 medium golden potato, boiled, at room temperature
    or cold
2 tablespoons canola oil
⅔ cup finely chopped onion
1 cup freshly boiled or canned beets, cut in ½-inch dices
4 slices tempeh bacon, chopped (see note)
1 teaspoon minced fresh rosemary,
    or ¼ teaspoon dried rosemary, crumbled
2 tablespoons ketchup
Salt and freshly ground pepper

NOTE

You will find tempeh bacon sold as Fakin' Bacon
in natural food stores.

1 Peel the potato and cut it into ¾-inch cubes.

2 In a heavy, medium skillet, heat the oil over medium-high heat. Sauté the onion until lightly browned, about 8 minutes, stirring often.

3 Mix in the beets, tempeh bacon, and rosemary. Add the potato and stir 1 to 2 minutes. The potato will break down slightly as it mixes with the other ingredients; this helps bind the hash together.

4 Mix in the ketchup. Season to taste with salt and pepper. Press the hash into a 1-inch thick layer and cook until it is brown and crusty on the bottom, about 5 minutes, reducing the heat if necessary.

5 Turn the hash over. It will break up, which is fine; the browned bits give it more flavor. Press the hash back into a 1-inch layer and cook to brown the bottom, about 5 minutes.

6 Remove the pan from the heat. Place a plate larger than the skillet over the pan. Placing your hand on the center of the plate, hold it firmly in place. Carefully lift the skillet and invert the pan so the hash falls onto the plate. Serve immediately. This dish can also be refrigerated or frozen and reheated in the oven. It will not be crisp-crusted, but it will taste delicious.

VARIATION

To give the hash an especially meaty quality, mix ⅓ cup TVP flakes into the sautéed onion before adding the beet and potato. It will make this seem more like roast beef than corned beef hash.

Carrot Flan with Pistachios

YIELD: 8 SERVINGS

Loaded with beta-carotene from the carrots, sweet red
peppers, and pumpkin seeds, this attractive dish is one of
the least obvious ways I know of serving tofu. It is perfect
when you are entertaining, not only because of its impressive
presentation but also because it can be made ahead of time.
Serve it either hot or at room temperature.

2 teaspoons canola oil
1 pound carrots
2 cups mild vegetable stock or water
¼ cup unsalted shelled pistachios
3 tablespoons whole wheat bread crumbs
½ fresh jalapeño pepper, seeded and chopped
1 yellow or orange bell pepper, roasted, peeled,
    and seeded, coarsely chopped
1 large shallot, minced (1½ tablespoons)
6 ounces firm or extra firm regular tofu, pressed
¼ cup chopped dill
Salt and freshly ground pepper

1 Preheat the oven to 350 degrees. Lightly oil the bottom and
sides of a 9-inch tart pan with a removable bottom.

2 Cut the carrots in half crosswise, making the top pieces
3½ inches long. Slice the bottom parts into thin rounds. Cut
the top portions lengthwise into ¼-inch slices.

3 In a medium saucepan, combine only the round slices with
the stock. Cook, covered, until they are very soft, 15 to
18 minutes. With a slotted spoon, remove the carrots and set

aside. Add the long carrot slices to the liquid in the pot. Cook, covered, until the carrots are crisp-tender, 5 minutes. Drain and set aside.

4 In the bowl of a food processor, combine the pistachios, bread crumbs, and jalapeño. Grind them to a fine meal. Sprinkle the mixture into the prepared tart pan. With your fingers, press the mixture firmly over the bottom of the pan to make a "crust" for the flan. Press some of the mixture into the ridges, reaching part-way up around the sides of the pan.

5 Wipe out the bowl of the food processor. Add the soft-cooked sliced carrots, roasted pepper, shallots, tofu, and dill. Process until finely ground. Season to taste with salt and pepper. Transfer this mixture to the prepared tart pan, spreading it out carefully over the crust to make an even layer.

6 Arrange the long, thin carrot slices over the pureed filling, overlapping them to make a sunburst pattern. Cover the center of the flan with 2 to 3 short pieces cut from 1 slice of carrot.

7 Brush the top of the flan with oil. Bake the flan 30 minutes in center of the oven. Let it cool in the pan 10 to 20 minutes. Slipping one hand under the pan, remove the ring to unmold the flan. Set it on a serving plate. Serve lukewarm or at room temperature.

VARIATION

• •

Replace the chopped fresh dill with ¾ teaspoon ground cumin. Its flavor gives this dish a whole different personality.

Korean Scallion-Stuffed Tofu

YIELD: 6 PIECES

Copeland Marks, in *The Korean Table*, says that Koreans eat small amounts of this spicy, simmered tofu dish, called *Tabu Choerim* as a garnish to flavor a big bowl of plain rice. But I find it easy to consume two pads of this fiery bean curd at a sitting because it is too good to stop at a few nibbles. If you wish, reduce the heat by cutting down on the amount of chili powder used. Enjoy this tofu hot or cold, cut up and added to a stir-fry or salad, or served as a light dish by itself.

16 ounces extra firm regular tofu
½ teaspoon kosher salt
3 tablespoons peanut or corn oil
¼ cup soy sauce
½ to 2 teaspoons hot red chili powder, or to taste (see note)
1 teaspoon sesame salt or *gomasio* (see note)
1 clove garlic, crushed to a paste
4 scallions, white and green parts, cut into 2-inch pieces
About 20 dried chile threads (optional but traditional;
      see note)

1 Cut the tofu horizontally in half. Cut it crosswise into thirds, making 6 pieces. With paper towels, pat the tofu slices dry. Sprinkle the salt over the tofu and let it stand for 10 minutes.
2 Heat the oil in a large skillet over medium heat and brown the tofu for about 3 minutes on each side. Drain on paper towels.
3 In a small bowl, combine the soy sauce, ¼ cup water, chili powder, sesame salt, and garlic. Put 1 tablespoon of the sauce

and one-third of the scallions on the bottom of a saucepan. Cover with 3 of the tofu slices in one layer; sprinkle with some sauce, another one-third of the scallions, and several red chile threads, if using. Add the remaining tofu to make a second layer, more chile threads, and the remaining sauce and scallions. Spread a few more chile threads on the top. Rinse the sauce bowl with 1 tablespoon of water and pour it over all.

4 Bring the liquid to a boil, cover the pan tightly, and simmer over low heat for 15 minutes to steam the tofu. Most of the liquid will evaporate. Serve warm or at room temperature, over rice, or use as an ingredient in other dishes. It will keep in a tightly closed container in the refrigerator for 4 to 5 days.

NOTES

Dried chili powder is ground red chile pepper. Chile threads are fine strips of dried red chile. Look for both in Korean food stores, or use cayenne in their place.

Japanese and natural foods stores sell sesame salt as the condiment called *gomasio*. Best when fresh, sesame salt is usually made from lightly dry-roasted sesame seeds (white or black) ground together with sea salt. This Korean version, offered by Copeland Marks, is even easier to make: Put 2 tablespoons sesame seeds and 1 teaspoon kosher salt in a mortar and pound them to a rough powder. Store in a jar with a tight cover and use when needed. Sprinkle a teaspoon of this seasoning on steamed spinach or broccoli.

Tomato-Braised Tofu

YIELD: 4 SERVINGS

On visits to California, I have become addicted to the Italian Braised Tofu made by Wildwood Natural Foods. Since this wonderful sweet-and-sour mélange is only available along the West Coast, I decided to duplicate the recipe so I can enjoy it regularly at home and share it with friends. This recipe shows how sautéing tofu in a minimum of oil can give the bean curd an appealingly chewy texture. Cold-pressed sesame oil (not to be confused with the pungent and dark toasted kind) adds a nutty note to the flavor of this dish.

2 tablespoons sesame oil
16 ounces firm or extra firm regular tofu, pressed and cut
        into ½-inch cubes
1 cup finely chopped celery
½ cup finely chopped onion
1 clove garlic, minced
2 teaspoons minced fresh ginger
¼ cup tomato paste
¼ cup natural soy sauce
2 tablespoons rice vinegar
2 tablespoons mirin rice wine
2 tablespoons rice syrup
2 teaspoons honey

1 In a large, heavy skillet, heat 1 tablespoon of the oil. Arrange half the tofu in 1 layer in the pan. Cook over medium-high heat until golden, 3 to 4 minutes. Turn and cook the tofu until it is golden on all sides. Turn the sautéed tofu into a bowl. Add the remaining oil to the pan and cook the remaining tofu. Transfer to the bowl using a slotted spoon.

2 In the same pan used for the tofu, cook the celery, onion, and garlic until the onion is translucent, stirring occasionally, about 5 minutes.

3 Meanwhile, in a bowl, combine the ginger, tomato paste, soy sauce, rice vinegar, mirin, rice syrup, and honey. Blend in 1 cup water.

4 Add the cooked tofu and the sauce mixture to the cooked vegetables in the pan and stir to mix. Simmer, uncovered, until the sauce is reduced by half, about 15 minutes.

5 Serve the braised tofu hot over brown rice, or let it cool and refrigerate until ready to use. Served at room temperature with toothpicks, this dish is good for snacking. Refrigerated, it keeps up to a week. It also can be frozen.

VARIATION

If you like hot food, give this dish a Tex-Mex kick by adding a minced serrano chile and $\frac{1}{3}$ cup diced plum tomato along with the celery, onion, and garlic.

Spinach Pesto

YIELD: 1 CUP

Italians call this a winter pesto, because it uses ingredients
easily found during the cold months, when fresh basil is not
available. Savory miso adds complex flavors different from
those of Parmesan cheese but just as appealing. Serve this
sauce on pasta as you would a traditional *Pesto Genovese*.
Also try it in mashed potatoes and on bruschetta. Use it
promptly, as the headiest notes in the miso do diminish
after a few hours.

3 cups spinach leaves (loosely packed), stemmed,
　　washed, and dried
1 cup Italian parsley leaves (loosely packed)
½ cup chopped walnuts
1 tablespoon sweet white miso
2 tablespoons brown rice miso
1 large clove garlic
¼ cup extra virgin olive oil
Salt and freshly ground pepper

1 In the bowl of a food processor, combine the spinach, parsley,
walnuts, white and brown miso, and garlic. Process until the
mixture is finely chopped, 2 to 3 minutes, stopping the motor
to scrape down the sides of the bowl once or twice.

2 With the motor running, gradually add 6 tablespoons of water,
1 tablespoon at a time. Still running the motor, drizzle in the
oil through the feeder tube in a thin stream. Scrape down the
sides of the bowl and taste the pesto. Season to taste with salt
and pepper. If you are waiting 2 to 3 hours to serve the pesto,
transfer it to a tightly covered container and do not refrigerate.

Spinach Baklava

Think of this dish as a light, crisp-crusted Greek lasagna.
Double the recipe, and you can freeze one pan of the baklava
to bake up another time. For a buffet meal, serve this with
the Red Peppers Stuffed with Millet, Corn, and Tempeh
(page 81), a platter of crudités surrounding a bowl of Aioli
(page 66), and a big green salad.

2 (10-ounce) packages frozen chopped spinach
5 tablespoons olive oil, or 1 tablespoon oil plus
    nonstick cooking spray
3 to 4 large scallions, white and green parts, thinly sliced
16 ounces firm or extra firm regular tofu, frozen and
    defrosted (see page 32)
½ cup golden raisins
½ cup tofu cream cheese
½ teaspoon ground cinnamon
⅛ teaspoon nutmeg
Grated zest of 1 small lemon (optional)
Salt and freshly ground pepper
16 sheets phyllo dough
Olive oil or nonstick cooking spray
1 cup whole wheat bread crumbs
½ cup grated soy or cow's milk Parmesan cheese

1 Preheat the oven to 400 degrees. Heavily coat a lasagna pan with nonstick cooking spray and set aside.

2 Cook the spinach just until it is defrosted and loses its raw taste, about 5 minutes. In a colander, drain the spinach. Run cold water over it to stop the cooking. Squeeze as much moisture as possible from the spinach. Place it in a large bowl and set aside.

3 In a medium skillet, heat 1 tablespoon of the oil over medium-high heat. Sauté the scallions until they are soft, 6 to 7 minutes, stirring often. Add the scallions to the spinach.

4 Crumble the defrosted tofu over the spinach and scallions. Add the raisins and mix until well combined. Mix in the cream cheese, cinnamon, nutmeg, and lemon zest, if using. Mix to blend. Season to taste with salt and pepper and set aside.

5 Lay a clean dish towel on the counter. Spread the phyllo out on the towel. Cover the phyllo with a lightly moistened, clean dish towel.

6 With a ruler, measure the bottom of the lasagna pan. Uncover the phyllo and, with a very sharp knife, cut the stacked sheets to the size of the pan. Replace the towel over the cut phyllo.

7 Lift one sheet of the dough and place it to cover the bottom of the prepared pan. Immediately cover the remaining stack of phyllo and keep it covered with the moist towel so the unused sheets of dough do not dry out as you work.

8 Lightly brush the phyllo in the pan with olive oil or spray it generously with nonstick cooking spray. Take care to cover the entire sheet. Sprinkle with 2 teaspoons of the bread crumbs and 1 teaspoon of the grated cheese. Cover with a second sheet of the phyllo. Repeat this procedure, continuing until 8 sheets of phyllo have been used. Do not sprinkle the top sheet with bread crumbs or cheese.

9 Spread the spinach and tofu mixture evenly over the layered phyllo.

10 Cover the filling with the remaining 8 sheets of phyllo, repeating the procedure of spraying it or brushing it with oil and sprinkling with bread crumbs and cheese. Coat the top of the baklava lightly with oil or cooking spray.

11 With a sharp knife, make 4 diagonal cuts in the top of the phyllo, spacing them about 2½ inches apart. Make 4 cuts in the other direction, making diamonds. Take care to cut only through the topmost layers of the phyllo: Do not press deeply enough to reach the filling, or the phyllo will separate too much during baking, making loose pieces.

12 Bake the baklava in the center of the oven until the phyllo is golden and crisp and a knife inserted in the center of the pan comes out clean, 30 to 35 minutes. Cool 10 to 15 minutes. Following the lines already made, cut in diamond-shaped pieces and serve hot or warm.

VARIATION

Instead of spreading the filling between layers of phyllo, use it to make a pie. I usually buy a package of frozen pie shells, put the filling in one, and roll out the second one to cut in strips to make a lattice top. Bake at 400 degrees for 30 minutes or until the pastry is golden.

Udon with Miso-Glazed Eggplant

Eggplant makes a perfect topping over plump Japanese *udon* noodles. You'll find this spaghetti-like pasta at both Japanese and natural food stores. The sauce, inspired by the sweet miso glaze used on *dengakee*, a grilled eggplant dish, goes perfectly with the pasta and creamy eggplant. If possible, use thin-skinned Japanese eggplant; they are more tender and taste sweeter than the Italian kind. You can skip using authentic Japanese ingredients like *dashi* (flavored broth) and *shichimi togarashi* (hot pepper), replacing them as indicated.

½ pound Japanese eggplant, or 1 small regular eggplant
3 tablespoons peanut oil
5 tablespoons aka miso (see note)
1 tablespoon hot *dashi* (see note), or vegetable broth
2 teaspoons *shichimi togarashi* (see sidebar),
    or ⅛ teaspoon cayenne
1 teaspoon balsamic vinegar
1 teaspoon grated orange zest
8 ounces *udon* noodles
½ cup hot *dashi* (see note) or vegetable broth
1 tablespoon finely sliced scallions

1 Cut the Japanese eggplant diagonally in ½-inch slices, then make 3 cuts at one end of each slice, creating a petal-like effect. For regular eggplant, cut in ¾-inch half moons.

2 Heat the peanut oil in a large, heavy skillet over medium-high heat. Add the eggplant in 1 layer. Cook 3 minutes, until the slices are golden-brown. Turn the slices and cook until the other side is browned, about 1 minute. Cover the pan, reduce the heat to medium, and cook until the eggplant is soft, about 6 minutes.

3 While the eggplant is cooking, make the sauce by combining the miso, 1 tablespoon *dashi*, *shichimi*, vinegar, and orange zest in a small pot. Cook over medium heat, stirring, until mixture is thick and glossy, about 5 minutes.

4 Cook the noodles, following the package directions. Drain, rinse in cold running water, and drain well. Divide the *udon* among 4 plates. Moisten each portion with 2 tablespoons of the hot *dashi*.

5 Spread about a teaspoon of the miso mixture on each slice of eggplant. Arrange one-quarter of the slices over each portion of noodles. Sprinkle with scallions and serve.

NOTES

Aka, or red, miso is sold at both natural and Japanese food stores. You can make *dashi* from recipes in *The Book of Miso* by William Shurleff and Akiko Aoyagi, or *Japanese Cooking, A Simple Art* by Shizuo Tsuji. Japanese food stores also sell instant *dashi*, as well as *shichimi togarashi*, a blend of seven peppers and seasonings.

Macaroni and Cheese au Gratin

YIELD: 6 SERVINGS

Macaroni and cheese has become the ubiquitous instant meal, usually thrown together out of a box. This version, made from scratch the way your grandmother might have prepared it, is not quick, but it is soulfully good. Make it when someone special needs soothing—especially you. I guarantee that preparing, as well as eating, this velvety, comforting dish will replenish you more than you can imagine.

2 cups macaroni
2 tablespoons unsalted butter or margarine
2 tablespoons all-purpose flour
1 cup plain regular soymilk, at room temperature
2 cups shredded soy Cheddar cheese
2 tablespoons whole wheat bread crumbs
2 tablespoons grated cow's milk or soy Parmesan cheese
½ teaspoon paprika
Pinch of cayenne
Salt and freshly ground pepper

1 Cook the pasta, following the directions on the package. Drain and set aside.
2 Meanwhile, preheat the broiler. Generously coat a shallow 6-cup ovenproof serving dish with 1 tablespoon of the butter or margarine and set aside.

3 In a medium saucepan, melt the remaining butter. Blend in the flour and cook over medium heat, stirring constantly with a wooden spoon, for 2 minutes. Reduce the heat, if necessary, to prevent the flour from browning. Gradually whisk in the soymilk, taking care to blend in each addition completely so the sauce stays smooth. Bring the sauce just to a boil and cook, whisking constantly 4 to 5 minutes, until it has the consistency of mayonnaise and loses its raw, floury taste. Mix in the Cheddar, stirring until it has melted. The sauce will be quite thick.

4 Mix the cooked pasta into the cheese sauce. Transfer the mixture to the prepared baking dish and smooth the top.

5 In a small bowl, combine the bread crumbs, Parmesan cheese, paprika, and cayenne. Season to taste with salt and pepper. Sprinkle the mixture evenly over the macaroni.

6 Place the baking dish under the broiler for 2 minutes until the bread crumbs are golden-brown, about 2 minutes. Serve immediately.

VARIATIONS

The possibilities seem endless, but here are some of my favorites. Use either smoked or jalapeño soy cheese in place of the Cheddar. Mix in ½ cup chopped roasted red bell pepper along with smoked cheese, or diced chopped jalapeño cheese. For Mac and Cheese Espagnol, mix in ½ cup each of sautéed chopped green bell pepper and onions, plus ½ cup well-drained chopped stewed tomatoes. I have even mixed cooked black beans and corn kernels into this mac and cheese, turning it into a Mexi-Mac casserole.

Pizzoccheri

YIELD: 4 SERVINGS

Pizzoccheri is both a dish from northern Italy and a kind of noodle made from buckwheat. Traditionally, the ingredients for this earthy one-dish meal are dark greens, potatoes, the pizzoccheri pasta, and sage, plus onions and a combination of cheeses. Here, the cholesterol-laden cheeses are omitted in favor of tempeh and a topping of soy Parmesan. In this particular recipe, the soy cheese works better than cow's milk Parmesan because of the way it melds with the other ingredients. Swiss chard tends to bleed, darkening the other ingredients in this dish, so serve it directly.

¾ pound Swiss chard
1 tablespoon olive oil
1 cup thinly sliced onion
1 large clove garlic, minced
1½ teaspoons rubbed sage
2 cups red-skinned potatoes, cut in ¾-inch dices
½ cup Roasted Vegetable Stock (page 60) or vegetable broth
4 ounces pizzoccheri pasta
4 ounces mild-flavored tempeh, such as quinoa and millet, or three-grain, chopped
4 tablespoons grated soy or cow's milk Parmesan cheese

1 Wash the chard and dry well. Fold each leaf in half lengthwise. Using the tip of your knife, cut lengthwise alongside the center spine of the leaf, trimming the leafy part from the stem. Set the leaves in one pile, stems in another.
2 Trim the bottom of the stems. Cut away and discard their upper part, keeping the wide lower portion of each stem. Slice the stems crosswise into ¾-inch pieces, about 1 cup. Set aside.

3 Stack the chard leaves on top of one another. Roll the piled leaves lengthwise, into a fat tube. Cut the rolled leaves crosswise into ¾-inch strips. You will have 7 to 8 loosely packed cups. Set aside.

4 Bring a 5-quart pot of water to a boil. Add the chard stems and cook until al dente, about 10 minutes. Drain and set aside.

5 Meanwhile, in a large, heavy skillet, heat the oil over medium-high heat. Add the onion and sauté until soft, 5 minutes. Stir in the garlic and sage; cook 1 minute more. Add the shredded chard leaves and potatoes. Mix in the broth. Bring the vegetables to a simmer, cover the pan, and cook until the chard is soft and the potatoes are al dente.

6 At the same time, boil a large pot of water and cook the noodles according to package directions.

7 Mix the cooked chard stems into the chard mixture and cook, uncovered, until the potatoes are lightly browned and soft. Mix in the tempeh and cook just until it is heated through.

8 Add the noodles to the cooked potato mixture; toss to blend. Turn onto a serving platter or 4 individual plates. Top with the grated cheese and serve immediately.

VARIATION

Instead of swiss chard, use cabbage cut in wedges and sliced crosswise into ¾-inch strips (about 6 cups). Mix in 8 ounces of pressed tofu in place of the tempeh, mixing it in at the end of cooking (at the same point as you would the tempeh). This version has a sweeter, milder flavor.

SIDE DISHES
AND SAUCES

SIDE DISHES AND SAUCES

*my favorite recipes

Miso-Glazed Carrots

YIELD: 4 SERVINGS

For some people, butter makes almost anything taste better:
I feel that way about miso. Here, its flavor is intensified by
the addition of two kinds of sesame oil: the pale, cold-pressed
kind and the dark, roasted Japanese type.

1 tablespoon cold-pressed sesame oil
¼ cup finely chopped onion
3 medium carrots, cut into ½-inch slices
1 tablespoon mellow white miso
¾ cup vegetable broth or water
2 teaspoons grated orange zest
1 teaspoon grated ginger root, or ½ teaspoon ground ginger
¼ teaspoon roasted sesame oil
Salt and freshly ground pepper

1 In a medium, heavy skillet over medium-high heat, heat the cold-pressed sesame oil. Add the onion and carrots. Sauté until the onion is soft, about 6 minutes, stirring occasionally. Take care not to let the onion color.

2 Meanwhile, in a small bowl, cream the miso with ¼ cup of the broth. Stir this mixture, the remaining broth, orange zest, and ginger into the carrots. Reduce the heat and simmer until the liquid is reduced to a glaze and carrots are crisp-tender, 12 to 15 minutes.

3 Stir in the roasted sesame oil and remove the pan from the heat. Season to taste with salt and pepper.

VARIATION

In place of carrots, use 1 medium sweet potato, peeled and thinly sliced, with the slices cut crosswise into half-moons. Cook until the sweet potatoes are soft but still hold their shape, about 15 minutes.

Sweet Bean and Corn Succotash

YIELD: 4 SERVINGS

Succotash was originally a Native American dish combining corn, beans, and squash. Today, it is most often just a blend of corn and lima beans. Once I tasted the Sweet Bean™, a vernally green, immature fresh soybean, I knew it would be perfect in succotash. It adds its high-quality protein and abundant fiber along with a flavor both nutty and sweet. Frozen shelled Sweet Beans made their debut in local supermarkets and natural food stores in 1996. They have long been sold in Chinese and other Asian food markets. In Japanese food shops, they are sold in the pod as *edamame*.

¼ cup finely chopped Spanish or sweet onion
1 cup Sweet Beans
1 cup corn kernels, fresh or frozen
1 scallion, white and green parts, sliced in ½-inch rounds
½ cup vegetable broth or water
1 tablespoon unsalted butter or margarine (optional)
Salt and freshly ground pepper

1 In a medium saucepan, combine the onion, Sweet Beans, corn, scallion, and broth and set the pot over medium-high heat. Bring to a boil, cover, and simmer until the beans have the texture of slightly undercooked baby lima beans. Mix in the butter, if using, until melted. Season to taste with salt and pepper and serve.

VARIATION

Add cooked brown rice and diced roasted red bell pepper to change this side dish into a main dish.

Miso Mashed Potatoes

YIELD: 4 SERVINGS

Yellow-fleshed potatoes, such as Yukon Gold or Yellow Finn, roughly mashed with chickpea miso is a marriage made in heaven. The texture of their skins against the creamy flesh of the potatoes adds to the pleasure of this dish. It's important to work quickly, while the potatoes are warm and moist.

1½ pounds yellow-fleshed potatoes
2 cloves garlic, peeled
2 tablespoons chickpea miso
1 tablespoon olive oil
Salt and pepper

1 In a medium saucepan, boil the potatoes with the garlic until the potatoes are soft when pierced with a knife, about 20 minutes.
2 Meanwhile, in a small bowl, using the back of a spoon, cream the chickpea miso together with the oil.
3 Drain the potatoes and garlic. As soon as they are cool enough to handle, peel half the potatoes and place them in a large bowl. Add the remaining unpeeled potatoes and the garlic cloves to the bowl. Scrape the miso mixture over the potatoes.
4 With a fork, roughly mash the potatoes, working the miso mixture into them. Leave the potatoes coarsely mashed with pieces of skin crumpled in. Season to taste with salt and pepper. Serve immediately.

VARIATION

It's almost gilding the lily, but sometimes I add lightly sautéed scallions browned in extra virgin olive oil.

Rich Miso Gravy

YIELD: 1 CUP

Light and dark miso, along with rich stock and lots of fresh mushrooms, give this gravy a meaty flavor that goes well with mashed potatoes, meatless meat loaf, and in casseroles. Leave in the mushrooms and pour the gravy over brown rice and steamed vegetables for a satisfying, light meal.

1 tablespoon canola oil
1 cup sliced white mushrooms
½ cup finely chopped onion
1 clove garlic, minced
⅓ cup dry red wine
2 cups Roasted Vegetable Stock (page 60)
1 tablespoon red miso
1 tablespoon sweet or mellow white miso

1 In a medium skillet, heat the oil over medium-high heat. Sauté the mushrooms, onion, and garlic until the mushrooms give up their liquid, about 5 minutes.
2 Add the red wine to the pan and cook until most of the liquid in the pan has evaporated and the mushroom mixture is just moist.
3 Pour in the stock. Boil until the liquid is reduced by half. Remove the pot from the heat.
4 In a small bowl, blend the two misos with 2 tablespoons of hot liquid spooned from the pan. Stir this miso mixture into the mushroom mixture. Strain the gravy, reserving the mushrooms to serve as a side dish, or use the gravy with the mushrooms in it, if you like.

VARIATION

If you have on hand soaking liquid left from porcini mushrooms, use it in place of up to 1 cup of the Roasted Vegetable Stock.

Creamy Miso Gravy

YIELD: 1¼ CUPS

In high school, I lived for the days the cafeteria served chicken croquettes and mashed potatoes blanketed in creamy gravy—the kind of thick sauce laden with fat and cholesterol that today we shun. Here is a dairy-free, miso-flavored gravy that seems as decadent as those old-fashioned sauces. To preserve the enzymes in the miso, take care not to let the gravy boil during cooking. Serve this velvety sauce over kasha, brown rice, or mashed potatoes.

2 teaspoons mellow miso
½ cup vegetable broth
½ cup plain regular soymilk
¼ teaspoon dried thyme
2 tablespoons canola oil
1 large clove garlic, quartered lengthwise
2 tablespoons minced onion
2 tablespoons all-purpose flour
Salt and freshly ground pepper

1 In a measuring cup or small bowl, cream the miso with ¼ cup of the broth. Add the remaining broth, the soymilk, and the thyme. Set aside.

2 In a small saucepan, heat the oil over medium-high heat. Sauté the garlic and onion until the onion is translucent, 2 to 3 minutes, stirring constantly.

3 Stir in the flour. Cook, stirring constantly, until the mixture loses its grainy texture, has the consistency of creamy peanut butter, and looks light beige. Reduce the heat if necessary, so the mixture does not brown.

4 Whisk in the miso–soymilk mixture all at once. Cook the gravy, stirring constantly, until it thickens, 2 to 3 minutes, taking care not to let it boil. Continue to cook while stirring for 3 minutes longer to help the flavors blend. Season with salt and pepper. Serve immediately or keep the gravy warm until ready to use.

VARIATION

Replacing the thyme with ½ teaspoon curry powder turns this gravy into a creamy curry sauce. To eliminate any raw taste from the curry powder, add it at the same time as the flour.

Tofu Sour Cream

YIELD: 1¼ CUPS

I much prefer this dairy-like blend to the cardboard flavor of commercially made fat-free dairy sour creams. The touch of lemon juice adds the fresh tang of sour cream and banishes any beany, "flat" flavor

1 (10½-ounce) package soft or firm silken tofu
2 teaspoons freshly squeezed lemon juice
¼ teaspoon salt

1 In a blender, puree the tofu. Blend in the lemon juice and salt. Transfer the tofu sour cream to a bowl and cover tightly. Chill 1 hour or until ready to use. If the cream thickens, restirring returns it to the texture of thick yogurt. Adjust the seasoning with salt and lemon juice before serving. This topping keeps 2 to 3 days in the refrigerator.

VARIATION

To make Dijon Mustard Tofu Cream, blend in 2 tablespoons Dijon mustard and use for making egg salad, as a spread on sandwiches, or as a condiment.

SALADS, BURGERS, AND KEBABS

SALADS, BURGERS, AND KEBABS

*my favorite recipes

Lentil Salad with Shallots and Miso Vinaigrette

YIELD: 6 SERVINGS

Chefs consider dark green LePuy lentils the aristocrat of lentils because of their velvety texture and spicy flavor. When imported from France, these lentils can cost as much as a pound of steak. Fortunately, thanks to growers in the United States who began importing French seed stock in 1994, you can now find them for less than a dollar a pound. The miso-sparked vinaigrette adds deep, smoky notes. The combination of flavors is so special that I often serve this salad as a party dish, particularly at buffets.

1 cup LePuy lentils
2 cloves garlic, peeled
1 small onion, halved
1 small carrot, cut in 4 pieces
½ cup finely chopped celery
1 tablespoon finely minced shallot
1 tablespoon red or hatcho miso
1 tablespoon red wine vinegar
1 tablespoon extra virgin olive oil
Salt and freshly ground pepper

1 In a medium saucepan, combine the lentils, garlic, onion, and carrot; add 2¼ cups water. Bring to a boil over high heat, cover, reduce the heat to low, and simmer until the lentils are al dente, 20 to 25 minutes.

2 Drain the lentils, reserving 2 tablespoons of their water. Place the lentils in a medium bowl. When they have cooled slightly, stir in the celery and shallots.

3 Prepare the dressing: In a small bowl, cream the miso with the reserved lentil cooking liquid and the vinegar. Mix in the olive oil. Pour the dressing over the warm lentils and toss with a fork to blend. Season to taste with salt and pepper. Serve warm or at room temperature.

VARIATION

Mix in 1½ cups finely diced smoked mozzarella or turkey.

Wild Rice and Smoked Tofu with Pecans and Currants

YIELD: 8 SERVINGS

Cubed smoked tofu tastes like nuggets of smoked turkey. A touch of roasted sesame oil accentuates the flavor of the tofu in this salad, while curry powder adds a lively counterpoint. This salad keeps well, making it a good choice for picnics. For a buffet table, garnish with a ring of red-skinned apple slices. This looks attractive and makes a good addition to the dish, as well.

2 cups cooked wild rice
¾ cup smoked tofu, cut in 1 by ¼-inch batons
¾ cup finely diced red bell pepper
½ cup finely diced yellow bell pepper
⅓ cup chopped pecans
¼ cup dried currants
1 large scallion, white and green parts, thinly sliced
½ teaspoon curry powder
⅛ teaspoon ground coriander
2 tablespoons fresh lemon juice
½ teaspoon salt
3 tablespoons canola oil
3 to 4 drops roasted sesame oil
Freshly ground pepper

1 In a medium bowl, combine the rice, tofu, peppers, pecans, currants, and scallion.

2 Prepare the dressing: In a small bowl, mix together the curry powder, coriander, lemon juice, and salt. Whisk in the canola oil and sesame oil. Season to taste with pepper. Pour the dressing over the salad and toss until well combined. In a tightly sealed container in the refrigerator, this salad keeps 1 to 2 days.

VARIATION

Instead of wild rice, use *wehani*, brown japonica, or any other nutty rice. A combination of wild and brown rice also works. In place of the peppers, diced apple and celery can be used.

Greek Salad with "Feta"

YIELD: 4 SERVINGS

Have you ever noticed the similarity between a block of bean curd and one of feta cheese? "What if tofu could be pickled, like feta," I thought one day. After much experimentation, here is a Greek salad topped with this brined soy "feta." Knowing cheese lovers would be skeptical, I served this salad beside one topped with a cow's milk feta bought at the supermarket. Taste this salad, and you'll know which version was preferred.

8 ounces firm or extra firm tofu, frozen and defrosted
    (see page 32)
2 tablespoons white vinegar
½ to 1 teaspoon kosher salt
½ pound tender fresh spinach, stemmed, washed, and dried
6 leaves red leaf lettuce, torn in pieces
6 leaves romaine lettuce, torn in pieces
12 slices cucumber
1 medium green bell pepper, seeded and cut into rings
1 medium tomato, cut in 8 wedges
1 hard-boiled egg, quartered
6 pickled peppers
¼ cup kalamata olives
6 anchovy fillets (optional)
2 very thin slices red onion
2 tablespoons red wine vinegar
2 tablespoons extra virgin olive oil
Salt and freshly ground pepper
¼ teaspoon dried oregano

1 Crumble the tofu into a bowl. Mix in the white vinegar and kosher salt. Cover and marinate in the refrigerator 45 minutes. Transfer the marinated tofu to a colander, rinse lightly with cold water, and set to drain while you assemble the salad.

2 On a large serving platter, arrange the spinach, red leaf lettuce, and romaine lettuce. Arrange the cucumber and green pepper over the greens. Place the wedges of tomato and egg nicely on top of them. Add the pickled peppers, olives, and anchovies, if using. Separate the onion into rings and arrange on top of the salad. Sprinkle the tofu feta over the salad.

3 Drizzle the red wine vinegar and oil over the salad. Season to taste with salt and pepper. Sprinkle the oregano over the salad. Toss and serve or set out the salad and let everyone help themselves.

VARIATION

Sometimes I stuff all the elements of this salad into a pita pocket—if you try this, be sure to use pitted olives!

Egyptian Parsley Salad

YIELD: 10 TO 12 SERVINGS

This salad makes a refreshing alternative to tabbouleh.
It offers a clever way to enjoy parsley, which is loaded with
vitamins and has fresh flavor that I think is unappreciated.

8 cups loosely packed coarsely chopped Italian parsley
    (about 3 large bunches)
1½ cups scallions, white and green parts, thinly sliced
    (1 bunch)
1½ cups finely chopped dill (1 large bunch)
1 small red onion, halved and cut lengthwise into thin slices
2 medium red bell peppers, halved and cut lengthwise
    into thin strips
5 cloves garlic, finely chopped
16 ounces firm or extra firm regular tofu,
    cut into ½-inch cubes (see note)
½ cup olive oil
¼ cup extra virgin olive oil
Juice of 2 lemons
2 teaspoons salt
Freshly ground pepper

NOTE

Pressed tofu will be chewier, but unpressed extra
firm tofu works nicely.

1 In a large bowl, combine the parsley, scallions, dill, onion, red pepper, garlic, and tofu.
2 Prepare the dressing: In a small bowl, whisk together the olive oils, lemon juice, and salt. Season to taste with pepper.
3 Pour the dressing over the salad and toss to combine. Adjust the seasoning to taste. Serve immediately.

VARIATION

Mix 3 to 4 cups of romaine lettuce leaves cut crosswise into ½-inch strips in with the rest of the salad. This makes a colorful green salad to serve with lasagna and other pasta dishes, or to put on a buffet table.

Eggless Egg Salad

YIELD: 4 SERVINGS

Since I loathe fake food, for years I looked down on so-called "eggless" salad made with tofu. Then I decided to make one that would satisfy my demanding taste. Frankly, I find this recipe a brilliant success. Using frozen tofu is important: Its texture really soaks up the flavor of the other ingredients.

8 ounces firm regular tofu, pressed, frozen, and defrosted
    (see page 32)
2 tablespoons finely chopped red onion
2 tablespoons sweet pickle relish
2 tablespoons soy mayonnaise
1 tablespoon fresh lemon juice
1 teaspoon dry mustard
½ teaspoon turmeric
½ teaspoon salt, or to taste
Freshly ground black pepper

1 In a medium bowl, combine the tofu, onion, pickle relish, mayonnaise, lemon juice, mustard, and turmeric. With a fork, mix until all the ingredients are blended together. Season to taste with salt and pepper. Cover with plastic wrap and refrigerate at least 1 hour to allow flavors to mellow, up to 24 hours. This salad keeps for up to 3 days in the refrigerator.

VARIATION

For crunchy eggless salad, substitute ¼ cup finely diced celery and 2 to 4 tablespoons finely diced sweet red pepper for the red onion and pickle relish. In place of mayonnaise, I use also add Dijon Mustard Tofu Cream (page 152) spiked with extra mustard.

Peanut Butter, Marmalade, and Miso Sandwich

YIELD: 2 SANDWICHES

Miso and peanut butter are perfect partners. Together, they go perfectly with the sweet and faintly bitter "edge" of orange marmalade. All together, I find this an addictive snack or light meal. Use the best imported English marmalade rather than the wimpy, fruit-sweetened kind. You'll appreciate the difference the moment you taste it.

¼ cup smooth peanut butter
1½ tablespoons sweet white miso
2 teaspoons peanut oil
4 slices cracked-wheat bread
4 to 6 tablespoons orange marmalade
2 leaves romaine lettuce

1 In a small bowl, blend the peanut butter and miso with the peanut oil.
2 Toast the bread. Spread 2 slices of bread with half the peanut-miso mixture.
3 Spread the marmalade thickly over the peanut-miso. Cover with the lettuce and remaining slices of bread. Cut the sandwiches in half and serve.

VARIATION

Apricot Butter (page 222) works nicely in place of the marmalade.

Real Russian Dressing

YIELD: 1/2 CUP

This creamy dressing has the zing missing from the pasty-tasting bottled stuff. Use this dressing on a crisp salad of romaine lettuce and on sandwiches (it really sparks up a cheese sandwich). For nostalgia's sake, try it on a wedge of iceberg lettuce or as a dip for shrimp and raw veggies.

1/2 cup soy mayonnaise (see note)
3 teaspoons chili sauce
1 tablespoon fresh lime juice
Freshly ground pepper

1 In a blender, combine the mayonnaise, chili sauce, and lime juice. Whiz until well blended. Season to taste with pepper.

NOTE

Soy mayonnaise is sold at natural food stores. It is made with tofu.

VARIATION

Mix in 1 tablespoon bottled white horseradish, well drained.

Creamy Ranch Dressing

YIELD: 1 CUP

Some prepared foods taste great until you read the ingredients on the package. That's when I decided to make a ranch dressing I could feel good about eating. Serve it on salads and as a dip.

1 scallion, white and green parts, cut in 1-inch lengths
2 large cloves garlic
2 teaspoons freshly squeezed lemon juice
1 tablespoon rice vinegar
½ teaspoon rice syrup
9 to 10½ ounces soft silken or regular tofu
1 teaspoon dried oregano
1 tablespoon canola oil
Salt and freshly ground pepper

1 In the bowl of a food processor, combine the scallion, garlic, lemon juice, rice vinegar, and rice syrup. Process by pulsing 5 to 6 times, then let the blade run about 10 seconds, until all the ingredients are very finely chopped. Scrape down the sides of the bowl. Add the tofu and process until the dressing is pureed. Add the oregano and oil and process just until they are blended into the dressing. Season to taste with salt and a generous amount of freshly ground pepper.

2 Let the dressing sit at least 10 minutes, up to 1 hour, to let the flavors meld. It keeps in a tightly closed container in the refrigerator for up to 3 days.

VARIATION
. . . .
Add ½ teaspoon coarsely ground black pepper to make Pepper Ranch Dressing.

Garlic Tempeh Croutons

YIELD: 1 CUP

Garlic lovers will wax ecstatic over the allium punch in these crunchy cubes. Along with flavor, these croutons provide a protein boost that turns a green salad into a main dish. Use them on a crisp greens, spinach salad, or sprinkled into a bowl of pea soup. Also enjoy them on pasta and steamed vegetables, and use them to deter vampires.

½ cup peanut oil
6 cloves garlic, halved lengthwise
4 ounces (½ package) three-grain or other
    mild-flavored tempeh

1 In a small, heavy saucepan over low heat, gently simmer the garlic in the oil for 15 minutes. It is important to keep the heat low enough so that the oil just bubbles and the garlic colors very little, if at all.
2 Let the garlic-infused oil cool for 30 minutes.
3 Meanwhile, preheat the oven to 450 degrees. Cover a wire baking rack with two layers of paper towels and set aside.

4 Cut away the rounded edges of the tempeh to form a flat-sided rectangle. Slice the tempeh horizontally in half, then cut it crosswise, making strips ⅜ inch wide. Cut each strip crosswise into ⅜-inch cubes. Keeping the cubes small helps the tempeh crisp better. Pour the unused oil into a glass jar, cover tightly, and keep refrigerated. (It is good used to make salad dressing and dribbled over cooked vegetables.)

5 In a food processor, puree the garlic and oil. The garlic will turn into pulpy bits. Pour half the oil, about ¼ cup, onto a jelly roll pan lined with foil. Add the tempeh and toss to coat the cubes with the oil.

6 Bake the tempeh on the center rack of the oven for 12 to 15 minutes, turning it once or twice to be sure it colors evenly. As soon as it is golden, remove the tempeh from the oven; if it gets too brown, it tastes acrid. With a slotted spatula, transfer the croutons to the rack covered with paper towels and drain. Pat the croutons with the towels to remove excess oil. Unless you love garlic fanatically, discard all the dark, bitter-tasting brown chunks of garlic. Serve warm.

NOTE

These croutons can be frozen and reheated.

VARIATION

Use just 2 cloves of garlic, plus 1 teaspoon of oregano to flavor the oil.

Nutty Mushroom Tofu Burgers

YIELD: 6 BURGERS

Portobello mushrooms plus whole wheat bread crumbs (sold at natural food stores) give these burgers plenty of flavor. Served on toasted whole-grain bread spread with honey mustard, they are an example of how vegan fare and soy cooking are moving into the mainstream because they taste so good.

8 ounces firm regular tofu
4 tablespoons olive oil
1 cup chopped onion
¾ cup chopped celery
1 clove garlic, minced
1⅓ cups chopped portobello mushrooms
1 teaspoon dried basil
½ teaspoon dried oregano
¼ teaspoon dried thyme
½ cup chopped walnuts
1 cup whole wheat bread crumbs
1 teaspoon fresh lemon juice
3 to 4 dashes hot pepper sauce
1 teaspoon salt
Freshly ground pepper
12 slices whole-grain bread
Honey mustard
Mayonnaise
6 crisp lettuce leaves

1 Cut the tofu into 4 chunks. Gently squeeze each piece until you have extracted as much moisture as possible. Crumble the tofu into a large bowl, breaking it into pieces the size of large-curd cottage cheese.

2 In a medium skillet, heat 3 tablespoons of the oil over medium-high heat. Sauté the onion, celery, and garlic until the onions are translucent, about 5 minutes. Add the mushrooms, basil, oregano, and thyme and sauté until the mushrooms give up their liquid, 3 to 4 minutes, stirring often. Keep cooking until the mixture holds together in the center of the pan. Add this mixture to the crumbled tofu.

3 Add the walnuts, bread crumbs, lemon juice, hot pepper sauce, salt, and pepper to taste to the tofu. Mix with a fork until all the ingredients are well blended. Using ½ cup at a time, form the mixture into six 3-inch patties. Wrap each patty in plastic wrap and refrigerate 1 hour or up to 24 hours.

4 To cook the burgers, heat the remaining oil in a nonstick skillet over medium-high heat. Cook the burgers until browned on one side. Turn and brown on the other side, until they are firm in the center when pressed.

5 Toast the bread. Spread honey mustard on six slices and spread mayonnaise on the other six. Place a burger on each slice spread with mayonnaise. Top with a lettuce leaf and the slice spread with honey mustard. Serve.

Lentil and Rice Burgers

YIELD: 8 SERVINGS

Somehow, the miso in these burgers brings all the other flavors into focus. I especially like these warm, moist burgers tucked into a pita pocket along with cool, crisp vegetables and a dollop of sharp Dijon Mustard Tofu Cream (page 152). Since these burgers are a bit delicate, the pita bread also lets you enjoy them neatly to the last bite.

4 tablespoons peanut oil
1 cup chopped onion
1 cup chopped green bell pepper
2 scallions, white and green parts, chopped
1 clove garlic, minced
1 teaspoon minced ginger root
1 cup cooked lentils
1 cup cooked brown short-grain rice
½ cup chopped cooked bok choy, spinach, or Swiss chard
1 cup whole wheat bread crumbs
2 tablespoons sesame seeds
2 tablespoons sunflower seeds
⅛ teaspoon cayenne
1 egg white, lightly beaten
2 tablespoons mugi miso
2 teaspoons natural soy sauce
¼ teaspoon roasted sesame oil
1 teaspoon salt
Freshly ground pepper

8 whole wheat pita, warmed
4 cups shredded lettuce
8 slices ripe tomato
Thinly sliced red onion
Dijon Mustard Tofu Cream (page 152)
Alfalfa sprouts

1 In a medium skillet, heat 2 tablespoons of the peanut oil over medium-high heat. Sauté the onion, green pepper, scallions, garlic, and ginger until the onion is translucent, about 5 minutes. Transfer the vegetables to a large bowl.

2 To the sautéed vegetables, add the lentils, rice, cooked green vegetable, and mix with a fork to blend. Mix in the bread crumbs, sesame and sunflower seeds, and cayenne. Blend in the egg white, miso, soy sauce, sesame oil, salt, and pepper to taste.

3 Lightly moisten your hands with water. Form the burger mixture into eight 3-inch patties, using about ⅓ cup of the mixture for each burger. As each patty is formed, place it on a nonstick baking sheet. When all the patties are made, cover the sheet with plastic wrap and refrigerate 1 to 4 hours to firm the burgers.

4 Brown the burgers well on both sides, using the remaining peanut oil in a nonstick skillet, 5 to 7 minutes in all.

5 To serve, open the pocket in the pita bread. Fill the pita with ½ cup of the lettuce. Add a slice of tomato, the burger, and some red onion rings. Spoon in a dollop of the Dijon Mustard Tofu Cream. Top with a tuft of the sprouts.

Incendiary Thai Kebabs

YIELD: 8 SKEWERS

This adaptation of Indonesian saté uses cubes of tempeh. The marinade is spiked with incendiary habanero chiles. Serve on a bed of fragrant jasmine rice, drizzled with soy sauce, and sweetened, Indonesian-style, with honey or sugar.

2 cloves garlic, minced
1 tablespoon minced fresh ginger root
1 to 2 habanero chiles, seeded and finely chopped
1 tablespoon dehydrated sugar juice or brown sugar
½ teaspoon salt
Freshly ground pepper
Juice of 2 limes
8 ounces (1 package) tempeh, cut in 1-inch cubes

1　In a small bowl, combine the garlic, ginger, chiles, sugar, salt, and a few grinds of the pepper. Mix in the lime juice and 2 tablespoons water.

2　Arrange the cubed tempeh in 1 layer in a shallow glass dish or plastic container. Pour the marinade over the tempeh. Cover and set aside for 1 hour, or refrigerate up to 24 hours (the longer the tempeh marinates, the hotter the kebabs will be).

3　Take eight 6-inch bamboo skewers and string 4 cubes of tempeh on each skewer. Discard the marinade. Grill, broil, or sear in a dry cast-iron skillet until just lightly blackened, turning promptly so the tempeh colors and cooks on all sides, about 10 minutes. Serve accompanied by your favorite soy or peanut dipping sauce.

VARIATION

. . . .

Stir-fry the marinated tempeh and serve it on a bed of shredded romaine lettuce, red onion, and sliced cucumber. Garnish with sprigs of fresh coriander, mint, and chopped scallions.

DESSERTS

DESSERTS

*my favorite recipes

Chocolate Silk Pie

YIELD: 8 TO 10 SERVINGS

With only three ingredients, this drop-dead dessert is a chocaholic's dream. It tastes sublime, takes only minutes to make, and contains zero cholesterol. The secret to success here is using top-quality chocolate. For me, that's Valrhona. But Caillebaut or Lindt Extra Fine are excellent, too. If you are a vegan, use a Dairy-Free Pie Crust (page 184). Use a frozen pie shell, and you can whip up this dessert in about ten minutes.

12 ounces semisweet or dark chocolate
12 ounces soft regular or silken tofu
1 teaspoon pure vanilla extract
1 (9-inch) pie shell, baked

1 Chop the chocolate into small pieces. Melt the chocolate in the top of a double boiler over hot water, stirring often.

2 While the chocolate is melting, puree the tofu in a food processor, stopping once or twice to scrape down the sides of the bowl with a rubber spatula. Add the melted chocolate and process until the tofu and chocolate are completely blended. Add the vanilla and pulse to blend.

3 Turn the chocolate mixture into the baked pie shell, spreading it with the spatula to fill the pie shell evenly.

4 To set the filling, refrigerate the pie 60 minutes. Let the pie stand at room temperature for 15 minutes, uncovered, before serving. This pie keeps 2 to 3 days in the refrigerator.

VARIATION

For utter decadence, carefully smooth the top of the pie before chilling. Meanwhile, melt 4 ounces of good quality dark chocolate. Spread it over the pie in an even layer. Chill to create a "crust." Melt 2 ounces white chocolate. Using a fork, drizzle this over the dark chocolate in swirls and zigzags. Refrigerate until just before serving.

Dairy-Free Pie Crust

YIELD: ONE 9-INCH DOUBLE-CRUST PIE OR
TWO 9-INCH PIE SHELLS

After trying innumerable recipes, I gave up on finding a satisfactory vegan pie crust. Those made with margarine tasted nasty, and the ones using oil were hopeless. Then, while talking with the people at Spectrum Naturals, Inc., they offered this recipe. It makes a buttery-tasting golden crust, thanks to their Spectrum Spread, a canola-based soft spread sold in natural food stores. Its crisp texture has a positive side: This crust does not get soggy. Use with cream pies and custardy fillings; it does not pair well with lighter, fruit fillings.

2½ cups unbleached all-purpose flour
Pinch of salt
⅔ cup Spectrum Spread
¼ cup ice water

1 Combine the flour and salt in a large bowl. Using a pastry cutter or your fingertips, work the Spectrum Spread into the flour until the mixture is crumbly, with pea-size pieces.
2 Work in the water 1 tablespoon at a time, until the mixture forms a ball. The dough will not be elastic but rather flaky, with some bits separating from the ball. Press the dough together firmly and wrap it tightly in plastic wrap. Chill at least 60 minutes before rolling out.

3 For rolling out: Divide the dough in half. On a lightly floured counter, roll out half to fit a 9-inch pie plate. This dough tends to be flaky. If it is hard to hold together, roll the dough out to a thick layer, transfer it to your pie plate, and press the dough into the desired thickness. Be sure enough dough extends over the edge of the pie plate so that you can seal it with a top crust or crimp with a decorative edge.

4 For baked pie shell: Preheat oven to 350 degrees. Prick the dough all over with the tines of a fork. Set an empty pie plate over the crust and fill it with pie weights, dried beans, or uncooked rice.

5 Bake the weighted crust for 20 minutes. Carefully remove the pie plate with weights and continue baking the crust 10 minutes more, until it is just firm to the touch and not dried out. It will be pale beige in color. Place on a rack to cool in the pan. When the pie shell is completely cool, fill it with the filling of your choice. Wrapped in foil, the baked shell keeps 1 to 2 days, unrefrigerated.

VARIATION

For Italian Cheese Pie, I make this pie crust using marsala and lemon zest. For this version, combine 1⅓ cups flour, a pinch of salt, and 1 teaspoon grated lemon zest with ⅓ cup Spectrum Spread. Add 1 tablespoon marsala and 1 to 2 tablespoons ice water, following the above method. Bake, using blind-baking directions above.

Italian Cheese Pie

YIELD: 8 TO 10 SERVINGS

The dense, fine texture of ricotta cheesecake, studded with
raisins and perfumed with marsala, inspired me to create this
dairy-free, no-bake pie. I owe thanks to Joyce Goldstein,
whose Italian cheesecake recipe showed me where to start,
and to the ladies at Bloodroot in Bridgeport, Connecticut, a
restaurant whose dairy-free desserts are legendary; the basic
method for making this pie is modeled after one of their
recipes. When you need to kick over the traces, have a wedge
of this pie as a light meal. It's a deliciously healthy way to
rebel.

1 (9-inch) Dairy-Free Pie Crust, baked, made using
    marsala variation (page 185)
⅔ cup golden raisins
⅓ cup marsala
4 ounces firm or extra firm regular tofu, cut in small cubes
¾ cup apple juice
1 tablespoon agar flakes
⅔ cup slivered blanched almonds
¼ cup unbleached cane sugar
Pinch of salt
1 tablespoon grated lemon zest
¾ cup canola oil
2 tablespoons fresh lemon juice
1 teaspoon pure vanilla extract
¾ cup pine nuts

1 In a small bowl, soak the raisins in the marsala for 10 minutes
to plump them. Drain well, reserving the soaking liquid, and
set aside.

2 In a small pot, combine the tofu, apple juice, and agar. Add the reserved liquid from the raisins. Bring just to a boil and reduce heat. Gently simmer until the agar flakes are entirely dissolved, about 15 minutes.

3 Meanwhile, in a food processor, combine the almonds, 1 tablespoon of the sugar, and the salt. Process until the almonds are finely ground.

4 With a slotted spoon, remove the tofu to a small bowl. Cover the pot to keep the cooking liquid from cooling. Quickly add one-third of the tofu and the lemon zest to the ground nuts. Process to blend. With the motor running, slowly drizzle ¼ cup of the oil into the nut mixture. Repeat, alternating the remaining tofu and oil until they are all combined. The mixture will have the grainy texture of ricotta cheese.

5 Add the lemon juice, vanilla, and remaining sugar and process to blend. With the motor running, gradually pour in the hot mixture. The filling will have the texture of thick mayonnaise and will remain slightly grainy. Stir the raisins into the mixture. Turn the filling into the pie shell and smooth the top.

6 In a 325-degree oven, roast the pine nuts until golden brown, about 15 minutes, stirring occasionally. Distribute the nuts in an even layer over the filling. To set the filling, refrigerate the pie, uncovered, for 60 minutes. If not serving the pie immediately, cover it with plastic. Before serving, let the pie stand at room temperature for 15 minutes.

VARIATION

For the holidays, I reduce the raisins to ½ cup and soak them in rum instead of marsala and add ¼ cup finely chopped candied fruit. Also, I use grated orange peel in place of the lemon zest.

Banana Coconut Bread Pudding

YIELD: 8 SERVINGS

Pureed banana, coconut milk, and a touch of rum add
to the appeal of this creamy custard. The Italian semolina
bread sold in the supermarket is perfect for this recipe,
sesame seeds and all. Just remember to discard the ends—or
munch on them while the bread soaks. Pudding lovers can
serve squares of this dessert warm, doused with flaming rum.

1 loaf semolina bread, torn in 1-inch pieces (about 8 cups)
1½ cups plain or vanilla regular soymilk
1 cup unsweetened coconut milk
½ cup raisins
2 tablespoons rum
2 medium bananas
1 egg, lightly beaten
½ cup unbleached cane sugar
1 teaspoon ground cinnamon
1 teaspoon pure vanilla extract
Pinch of salt

1 Place the bread in a large bowl. Pour the soymilk and coconut milk over it and mix with a fork until the bread is completely moistened. Set aside for 30 minutes.

2 In a small bowl, soak the raisins in the rum for 25 to 30 minutes.

3 Preheat the oven to 350 degrees. Butter a 9-inch square baking pan or spray it generously with nonstick cooking spray. Place a rack in the center of the oven.

4 In a blender, puree the bananas. Add to the soaked bread, along with the egg, sugar, cinnamon, vanilla, and salt. Add the raisins and their soaking liquid. With a fork, mix until all the ingredients are well combined. Turn the pudding into the prepared pan. Spread it into an even layer.

5 Bake the pudding in the center of the oven 30 minutes. When it is done, it will be set and firm to the touch except in the middle, where it remains moist. Cool to lukewarm before cutting into 8 servings.

VARIATION

Use ½ cup pineapple juice in place of half of the coconut milk, and replace the raisins with currants. This variation makes the pudding lighter and further heightens its tropical taste.

Double Chocolate Pudding

YIELD: 4 SERVINGS

Homemade pudding is usually cozy and comforting. This one is so smooth and intense that it comes on more like a hausfrau who's traded her apron for black lace. For best results, use the best quality chocolate and a premium cocoa.

3 tablespoons unsweetened cocoa (Dutch-processed)
3 tablespoons arrowroot powder
½ cup unbleached cane sugar
⅛ teaspoon salt
2 cups plain regular soymilk
2 ounces bittersweet chocolate, finely chopped
1 teaspoon pure vanilla extract

1 Sift together the cocoa and arrowroot powder to remove all lumps. In a small saucepan, combine the cocoa, arrowroot powder, sugar, and salt, stirring them with a wooden spoon. Blend in ½ cup of the soymilk, stirring to make a smooth paste.

2 Gradually stir in the remaining soymilk. Place the pot over medium heat and cook, stirring constantly until the mixture boils. Reduce the heat and simmer until the pudding thickens, 2 to 3 minutes, stirring constantly. Remove the pot from the heat.

3 Mix the chopped chocolate into the hot pudding until the chocolate has melted completely. Gently blend in the vanilla.

4 Pour the pudding into 4 dessert dishes or small bowls. Cover with plastic wrap, making sure the plastic touches the surface of the pudding to prevent a skin from forming. Let the pudding come to lukewarm before serving, or chill.

VARIATION

If you prefer milk chocolate, substitute a good quality Swiss, Belgian, or French milk chocolate for the 2 ounces of bittersweet. Be sure to use a top-quality Swiss or Belgian brand. This version will be sweeter, with a softer chocolate flavor.

Apple Cranberry Crumble

YIELD: 8 SERVINGS

On a chilly, wet day, hot soup followed by a bowl of this dessert is just the thing. The hearty topping, soymilk, and fruit make the crumble suitable as a light meal when you want a break in routine. (It's great for breakfast.) Use only regular rolled oats; the thinner, quick cooking or instant kinds do not produce a crisp topping.

Filling

2½ pounds Granny Smith apples, peeled, cored, and
    cut into ½-inch slices
½ cup dried cranberries
½ cup unbleached cane sugar
¼ teaspoon freshly grated nutmeg
1 cup plain or vanilla regular soymilk

Topping

¾ cup regular rolled oats (not quick or instant)
⅔ cup all-purpose flour
¼ cup soy flour
¾ cup dehydrated sugarcane juice or dark brown sugar
1 teaspoon ground cinnamon
½ cup cold unsalted butter or margarine, cut in bits, or
    Spectrum Spread

1 Preheat the oven to 375 degrees. Grease an 8-cup, deep baking dish.

2 Prepare the filling: In a large bowl, combine the apples, cranberries, sugar, and nutmeg. With your hands, toss until the apples are well coated with the sugar and spice. Turn the fruit into the prepared baking dish and arrange in an even layer. Pour the soymilk over the fruit.

3 Prepare the topping: In a large bowl, combine the oats and both flours. Mix in the sugar and cinnamon. Using a fork, blend in the shortening until the mixture is well blended. With your fingers, pat the topping over the fruit to form a crust. (While it's nice to cover as much of the apples as possible, it is not essential.)

4 Bake the crumble until the topping turns golden and the apples are tender when a knife is inserted, about 40 minutes. Let the crumble sit 15 to 20 minutes before serving.

VARIATION

Use pears in place of the sliced apples; Bartletts are best.

The Creamiest Tofu Cheesecake in the World

YIELD: 8 SERVINGS

If you like rich New York-style cheesecake, here is a dreamy version. Touched with lemon, it contains far less cholesterol than conventional cheesecake, while not compromising a whit on taste or texture. The secrets of its success are using tofu cream cheese and silken tofu, plus arrowroot powder, which absorbs some of the moisture from the tofu while adding creaminess. If your natural food store does not have tofu cream cheese, check the local deli or bagel shop. They often sell it in bulk. Supermarkets and specialty food stores sell arrowroot powder in the spice section. Natural food stores often sell it too—and less expensively.

Crust
1 cup graham cracker crumbs
½ cup finely ground almonds
¼ cup sugar
4 tablespoons unsalted butter or margarine, melted, or Spectrum Spread

NOTE

The cake tastes delicious as soon as it is chilled through, but it reaches full creaminess only after being refrigerated 8 hours or overnight. For the crust, use regular sugar or it will have a gritty texture.

Filling

16 ounces soft silken tofu

16 ounces tofu cream cheese

¾ cup unbleached cane sugar

2 eggs

4 teaspoons grated lemon zest

2 tablespoons fresh lemon juice

½ teaspoon pure vanilla extract

2 tablespoons arrowroot powder

1 Preheat the oven to 350 degrees.

2 Prepare the crust: In a bowl, combine the graham cracker crumbs with the ground almonds and sugar. With a fork, blend the butter into the mixture until it clings together when you press a teaspoon of it between your fingers. Turn half the mixture into a 7-inch springform pan. With your fingers or the back of a soup spoon, spread and pat the crust until it covers the bottom of the pan. Spoon the remaining crust mixture around the sides of the pan with your fingers, pat the mixture and press it, working the crust up the sides of the pan to a height of about 2 inches, leaving it thicker around the bottom edge where the sides and bottom of the pan meet. Make the crust thinner around the top edge. Set it in the refrigerator while you make the filling.

3 Prepare the filling: Puree the tofu in a food processor. Add the cream cheese and process to blend. Add the sugar and eggs and process to incorporate them completely. Blend in the lemon zest, lemon juice, and vanilla. Blend in the arrowroot.

4 Pour the filling into the prepared crust, filling it to within $\frac{1}{2}$ inch of the top. Bake in the center of the oven for 50 to 60 minutes. The cake will be lightly colored on top. It may be slightly browned around the edges. It should jiggle in the center. Turn off the heat but leave the cake sitting in the oven for 60 minutes. (It is okay to peek quickly once or twice.) The top of the warm cake will be golden to lightly browned and just soft to the touch in the center. Set the cake on a rack and let it cool to room temperature. Cover the cake with foil and refrigerate in the pan overnight before serving.

VARIATION

For me, changing this recipe would be tampering with perfection, but if you have suggestions, let me know.

Mincemeat Croustade

YIELD: 8 SERVINGS

In the Auvergne region in southwestern France, plump prunes are the traditional filling for this turban-shaped dessert. One Thanksgiving, I decided to try a mincemeat filling; it worked perfectly. Then I discovered that blending a bit of miso into the mincemeat both adds flavor and speeds its ripening. Brandy Velvet Dessert Topping (page 206), a drizzle of pureed raspberries, or chocolate sauce adds a nice flourish to this dessert.

2 cups dried currants
¾ cup raisins
¾ cup golden raisins
2 Golden Delicious apples, peeled and cored, finely chopped
1 cup sliced almonds
1 teaspoon ground cinnamon
¼ teaspoon ground cloves
¼ teaspoon ground allspice
½ cup chopped candied orange peel
Zest of 1 orange, finely minced
Zest of 1 lemon, finely minced
1 tablespoon hatcho miso
⅓ cup dark rum
16 sheets phyllo dough
⅓ cup melted butter, mild-flavored olive oil, or butter-flavored cooking spray

1 Prepare the mincemeat: In a large bowl, combine the currants, raisins, golden raisins, apple, and almonds.

2 Rinse the candied orange peel, drain, and pat dry; add it to the fruit and nut mixture. Add the orange zest, lemon zest, and the spices. With a large rubber spatula, mix together the fruits, nuts, and spices until well combined.

3 In a small bowl, cream the miso with the rum, mixing until the miso is entirely dissolved. Blend this mixture into the mincemeat. Pack the mincemeat into a large plastic container or glass jar. Cover tightly and refrigerate overnight or up to a week, so the flavors can meld.

4 Preheat the oven to 400 degrees.

5 Assemble the croustade: On a baking sheet, place 2 sheets of the phyllo, positioning them horizontally with the left half of the sheets overhanging the side of pan. Brush with the butter or oil or spray with cooking spray. Quickly working clockwise, place 2 more sheets of the phyllo at a 10 o'clock position and brush or spray. Repeat, until 8 double sheets of phyllo radiate out in a large circle, with all the layers of phyllo overlapping in the center of the pan working as rapidly as you can. Heap 6 cups of mincemeat in the center of the dough. Spread it to cover the dough in a 10-inch circle.

6 Working counterclockwise, slip your hand under the topmost 2 sheets of phyllo (in the 8 o'clock position). Bring the dough in towards the middle, gathering it and leaving the ends pointing straight up at the center of the croustade. Working rapidly around the circle, repeat until the filling is encased in overlapping sheets of phyllo. With your fingers, gently twist the upstanding phyllo ends to form a topknot in the center of the croustade. Don't worry if some dough is brittle and breaks off.

7 Brush the croustade lightly with the melted butter or spray it with cooking spray. Place the croustade, on its baking sheet, in the oven. Bake until the croustade is golden and the edges of the topknot are nicely browned, 25 to 30 minutes. If you want to transfer the baked croustade to a serving plate, lift it gently, using two large pancake turners slipped underneath from opposite sides. Ideally, have someone hold the baking pan with the croustade just over the serving platter while you insert the turners. Have the other person slowly pull the pan from under the croustade, so you can lower it onto the plate. Serve warm or at room temperature, cut in wedges.

VARIATIONS

Use the filling for a traditional mincemeat pie or to stuff baked apples. Warmed, it's a good topping to serve over ice cream. Also, instead of the mincemeat filling, make a croustade filled with sliced apples tossed with brown sugar, walnuts, and cinnamon.

Indian Pudding

YIELD: 6 TO 8 SERVINGS

When I was young, The White Turkey restaurant in
New York City served Indian Pudding topped with vanilla
ice cream. The memory of the warm, grainy pudding bathed
in melting ice cream still lingers. Thanks to *Classic Home
Desserts* by Richard Sax for showing the best method for
making the kind of Indian Pudding I recall. Brandy Velvet
Dessert Topping goes nicely on this dessert, or try some
ice cream.

3½ cups plain or regular soymilk
½ cup cornmeal
1 egg, lightly beaten
¼ cup unsulfured molasses
2 tablespoons maple syrup
½ cup golden or regular raisins
1 teaspoon ground cinnamon
¾ teaspoon ground ginger
¼ teaspoon ground nutmeg
⅛ teaspoon ground cloves

1 Preheat the oven to 275 degrees. Spray a 2-quart soufflé dish
or 8-cup baking dish generously with nonstick cooking spray.
2 Pour ½ cup of soymilk into a small bowl. Whisk in the cornmeal. Set aside.
3 In a heavy, medium saucepan, heat 2½ cups of the soymilk
until the surface jiggles; do not boil.

4 Whisk the soaked cornmeal into the hot liquid, breaking up any lumps that form. Keep whisking or stir with a wooden spoon for 10 minutes, taking care that the cornmeal does not stick to the bottom of the pot. Remove the pudding from the heat. When the cornmeal has thickened to the consistency of Cream of Wheat, about 5 minutes, pour the mixture into the prepared baking dish.

5 In a bowl, whisk together the egg, molasses, maple syrup, raisins, cinnamon, ginger, nutmeg, and cloves. Stirring vigorously, blend this mixture into the cornmeal.

6 Let the pudding sit for 3 minutes, until the top sets. Place the baking dish on a rack in the center of the oven. Gently pour the remaining ½ cup of soymilk over the pudding. Bake 2½ hours, until a knife inserted in the center of the pudding comes out clean. Serve warm in individual bowls, topped with a small scoop of vanilla ice cream, if desired.

VARIATION

For breakfast, I like a chunky version of this dessert. To make it, add 1 medium apple, peeled, cored, and chopped, along with the raisins. Check this version after it has baked for 2 hours, as it may set faster than the regular recipe. Cool to room temperature and refrigerate. To reheat, cut the pudding into 1½-inch slices and heat in a nonstick skillet or microwave. Serve with maple syrup.

Gingerbread

YIELD: 2 LOAVES

This hot water gingerbread has a light, fluffy crumb. Be sure to slice this cake thickly, or it will fall apart. It freezes well, so put away the second loaf if you don't need it for a while.

2¼ cups unbleached all-purpose flour
¼ cup soy flour
1 tablespoon baking soda
½ teaspoon double-acting baking powder
2 teaspoons ground ginger
1½ teaspoons ground cinnamon
1 teaspoon unsweetened cocoa (Dutch-processed)
½ teaspoon ground cloves
¼ teaspoon ground black pepper
2 eggs
¾ cup unsulfered molasses
¾ cup packed dark brown sugar
¾ cup unsalted butter, melted
1 cup boiling water

1 Preheat the oven to 350 degrees. Place a rack in the center of the oven. Grease two 8-cup loaf pans. Flour the pans and line them with baking parchment.

2 In a bowl, combine the all-purpose and soy flours, baking soda, baking powder, ginger, cinnamon, cocoa, cloves, and pepper.

3 In a large bowl, lightly beat the eggs. Mix in the molasses, brown sugar, and melted butter.

4 Add the dry ingredients to the wet in two batches, mixing briskly until they are well combined before adding the next batch. Stir in the butter. Pour in the boiling water and mix well.

5 Divide the batter evenly between the 2 prepared pans. Bake for 30 to 40 minutes, until a knife inserted in the center comes out clean. Turn the loaves of gingerbread out onto a rack. Remove the baking parchment. Let the cakes cool partially. While they cool, make the topping. Slice and serve lukewarm, topped with Spiced Peach Topping (page 207) or Orange Dessert Topping (page 205).

Creamy Dessert Topping

YIELD: ABOUT 1 CUP

When a dessert calls for a dollop of whipped cream, try this topping instead. Using a mild-tasting silken tofu is important. Enjoy this topping on fresh berries, fruit compote, and shortcake.

8 ounces or 1 (10½-ounce) package soft silken tofu
2 teaspoons maple syrup
1 teaspoon fresh lemon juice
¼ teaspoon pure vanilla extract

1 In a blender or food processor, puree the tofu. Add the maple syrup, lemon juice, and vanilla and blend well. Transfer the topping to a bowl or plastic container and cover tightly.
2 Chill for 60 minutes or until ready to serve. If the topping thickens, stirring will return it to the texture of yogurt. It keeps 2 to 3 days in the refrigerator.

Orange Dessert Topping

YIELD: ABOUT 1 CUP

The orange juice tints this topping to a lovely apricot color. Enjoy it on strawberries, blueberries, and on gingerbread.

8 ounces or 1 (10½-ounce) package soft silken tofu
2 tablespoons orange juice concentrate
1 teaspoon fresh lemon juice
1 teaspoon Grand Marnier

1 In a blender or food processor, puree the tofu. Add the orange juice concentrate, lemon juice, and Grand Marnier and blend well. Transfer the topping to a bowl or plastic container and cover tightly.
2 Chill for 60 minutes or until ready to serve. If the topping has thickened, stirring will return it to the texture of yogurt. It keeps 2 to 3 days in the refrigerator.

Brandy Velvet Dessert Topping

YIELD: ABOUT 1 CUP

This topping has the rich color of pale coffee and cream. It goes nicely with Indian Pudding (page 200) and Mincemeat Croustade (page 197). You can also enjoy it on fruit compote and baked fruit.

1 (10½-ounce) package firm silken tofu
3 tablespoons dark brown sugar
1 tablespoon brandy
1 teaspoon fresh lemon juice

1 In a blender or food processor, puree the tofu. Add the sugar, brandy, and lemon juice and blend well. Transfer the topping to a bowl or plastic container and cover tightly.

2 Chill 60 minutes or until ready to serve. If the topping thickens, stirring will return it to the texture of yogurt. It keeps 2 to 3 days in the refrigerator.

VARIATION

In place of the brandy, you can flavor this topping with Calvados or rum.

Spiced Peach Topping

YIELD: 8 SERVINGS

While this topping is perfect on gingerbread, it goes well with many other desserts—and on pancakes or French toast at breakfast, too. Fresh peaches often have so little flavor that I've found frozen fruit often tastes as good.

1 tablespoon unsalted butter
¼ cup orange juice
2 tablespoons brown sugar
2 tablespoons maple syrup
¼ teaspoon ground cinnamon
1 teaspoon pure vanilla extract
1 (20-ounce) bag unsweetened frozen sliced peaches,
    or 2½ cups ripe fresh peaches, sliced

1 In a medium skillet with a tight-fitting lid, melt the butter over medium-high heat. Stir in the orange juice, sugar, maple syrup, cinnamon, and vanilla. Simmer just until the sugar dissolves, stirring as needed.

2 Add the peaches. Cover the pan and simmer 4 to 5 minutes. If using frozen peaches, uncover and separate the peach slices. Stir to help the fruit cook evenly. Replace the cover and cook until the peaches are al dente, 7 to 8 minutes.

3 Remove the cover and cook until the liquid in the pan is the consistency of milk. Serve warm, over squares of gingerbread, spice cake, or ice cream.

VARIATION

Mix in a cup of fresh blueberries when they are in season, at the same time as the peaches.

BREAKFAST AND
BEVERAGES

BREAKFAST AND BEVERAGES

*my favorite recipes

Stuffed French Toast

YIELD: 4 TO 8 SERVINGS

French toast is always special, but this bit of culinary trompe l'oeil really stands out. The inexpensive semolina bread sold at the supermarket is perfect for making this recipe. You can make this French Toast ahead, wrap each portion in foil, and freeze it. Just reheat it in the oven to serve. In fact, I often make a double batch, one for company brunch and one for me. Using a toaster oven, I can then effortlessly reward myself with a special breakfast by heating up a slice anytime.

¼ cup raisins

¼ cup golden raisins

¼ cup currants

¼ cup candied orange peel or candied fruit without cherries

½ cup brandy or rum

1 (1-pound) loaf Italian semolina bread

16 ounces regular firm or extra firm tofu, frozen and
        defrosted (see page 32)

2 teaspoons grated orange or lemon zest

3 eggs

1 cup plain or vanilla regular soymilk

1 teaspoon pure vanilla extract

3 tablespoons melted unsalted butter or
        nonstick cooking spray

1 In a small bowl, combine the raisins, golden raisins, currants, and candied peel with the brandy. Set aside to soak for 30 minutes.

2 Slice the bread diagonally into 1-inch slices, discarding the ends. Carefully pull the center from each slice, leaving about a ½ inch of bread inside the crust. Set aside the rings of crusts.

Tear the centers into ½-inch pieces and place them in a large bowl.

3 Crumble the tofu into the bowl with the torn bread, breaking it into bits the size of cottage cheese curd. Drain the dried fruit and add it to the bowl. Add the citrus zest.

4 In another large bowl, beat the eggs with the soymilk and vanilla. Pour half this mixture into the bowl with the torn bread. Stir with a fork until the bread is moistened and all the ingredients are well combined.

5 In batches, add 2 to 3 of the bread rings to the remaining egg mixture, turning the pieces once when they are well moistened.

6 Heat half the butter or oil in a large, heavy skillet over medium-high heat, or spray the pan with nonstick cooking spray before placing it over the heat. Arrange the soaked bread rings in the pan. Spoon the moistened bread and fruit mixture into the center of each ring, pressing with the back of the spoon to pack it firmly. Cook until the toast is browned on the bottom, 3 to 4 minutes. With a spatula, turn and brown the second side. Remove to a warm platter. Repeat until all the bread has been stuffed and cooked. Serve at once, accompanied by maple syrup or sprinkled with confectioners' sugar. Or, let the slices of stuffed toast cool. Wrap tightly in foil and freeze. To reheat, set in a 350-degree oven, wrapped in foil, 15 to 20 minutes.

VARIATION

Use ½ cup each dried blueberries and chopped dried cranberries in place of the raisins, currants, and candied fruit. Plump the fruit in Grand Marnier or Triple Sec.

Breakfast and Beverages

Chocolate Pancakes

YIELD: FOURTEEN 3-INCH PANCAKES; 4 TO 7 SERVINGS

Chocolate for breakfast sounds decadent, but it's sensible and healthy with these soy-and-cocoa flapjacks. Fresh strawberries are the perfect accompaniment, though some people prefer maple syrup or vanilla yogurt. Since they freeze beautifully, keep some of these pancakes in the freezer, ready to pop in the oven or toaster. The batter also makes crisp waffles.

1⅓ cups unbleached all-purpose flour
½ cup unsweetened cocoa (Dutch-processed)
2 teaspoons double-acting baking powder
2 tablespoons sugar
3 large eggs
3 tablespoons melted unsalted butter or canola oil
1½ cups plain regular soymilk
Pinch of salt
1 pint fresh strawberries, hulled and sliced (optional)

1 Sift the all-purpose and soy flours, the cocoa, and baking powder together into a medium bowl. Whisk in the sugar.

2 In another bowl, lightly beat the eggs. Whisk in the butter or oil, soymilk, and salt until well combined.

3 Add the wet ingredients to the dry ingredients, mixing just until they are blended together. The mixture will be slightly lumpy and have the consistency of cake batter.

4 Spray a cast-iron skillet with nonstick cooking spray. Place the pan over medium-high heat. Ladle the batter by scant ¼ cups into the pan. Cook until bubbles form on the surface and the edges darken, about 2 minutes. Turn and continue cooking until the pancake resists lightly when gently pressed in the center with your finger, about 2 minutes. Repeat until all the batter is used up. Keep the cooked pancakes covered and warm in a low oven until they are all ready to serve. Serve, accompanied by sliced strawberries, if you wish.

VARIATION

Make an ice cream sandwich by spreading vanilla ice milk between 2 of these pancakes. Wrap in plastic and freeze. Unwrap and enjoy!

Breakfast and Beverages

••••

215

Breakfast Rice Pudding

YIELD: 8 SERVINGS

If you avoid breakfast, this naturally sweet "pudding" may change your mind—and your habit of skipping the most important meal of the day. I make this in the evening and refrigerate it overnight. In the morning, it is firm and easy to cut into squares, which you can take along to eat while on the move. Some days, I take a second helping of this pudding after dinner with a dollop of Brandy Velvet Dessert Topping (page 206).

½ cup dried cherries
1 tablespoon cornstarch
2 cups plain or vanilla regular soymilk
¼ cup maple syrup
1 teaspoon pure vanilla extract
2 eggs, lightly beaten
1½ cups cooked brown rice
½ cup dried currants

1 Preheat the oven to 350 degrees. Spray an 8-cup pan generously with nonstick cooking spray.

2 In a small bowl, just cover the cherries with hot water and soak until they are soft, about 10 minutes. Drain well and set aside.

3 Place the cornstarch in a large bowl. Whisk in the soymilk, maple syrup, and vanilla. Beat in the eggs until well mixed.

4 Stir the rice, soaked cherries, and currants into the soymilk mixture. Pour into the prepared baking dish.

5 Set a large, deep pan (such as a roasting pan) on a rack in the center of the oven. Set the pan with the pudding in the center of the larger pan. Pour hot water into the large pan until the level of the water is halfway up the sides of the pan containing the pudding. Bake until a knife inserted in the center of the pudding comes out clean, about 1 hour and 15 minutes. Cool to lukewarm and serve, or cool completely, cover with plastic wrap, and refrigerate. This pudding keeps 3 to 4 days—if it lasts that long.

VARIATIONS

Use cooked wild rice in place of part of the brown rice. Or try cooked millet in place of the rice. (Millet is a light grain that's particularly nice in hot summer weather.) Substitute dried cranberries or blueberries for the dried cherries.

Zucchini Muffins

YIELD: TWELVE 3-INCH MUFFINS

Soy flour adds extra nutritional goodness to these light, fragrant muffins. Because this flour colors easily, these muffins bake at 350 degrees instead of the higher oven temperature used for most muffin recipes.

1¼ cups unbleached all-purpose flour
¼ cup soy flour
1½ teaspoons cinnamon
¾ teaspoon baking soda
¼ teaspoon double-acting baking powder
½ teaspoon salt
½ cup canola oil
1 teaspoon pure vanilla extract
1 egg
1 cup unbleached cane sugar
1½ cups finely shredded zucchini
½ cup chopped walnuts
½ cup golden raisins

1 Preheat the oven to 350 degrees. Lightly grease a 12-cavity muffin tin with butter, margarine, or nonstick spray and set aside.

2 In a medium bowl, whisk together the flour, soy flour, cinnamon, baking soda, baking powder, and salt until combined. Set aside.

3 In a small bowl, combine the oil, vanilla, and ½ cup cold water.

4 In a large bowl, using a hand-held mixer, lightly beat the egg. Gradually beat in the sugar. Continue beating until the mixture is lemon in color and thickened. Mix in the zucchini. Blend in the oil mixture.

5 Quickly stir the flour mixture into the batter, using as few strokes as possible. Before the dry ingredients are entirely moist, fold in the walnuts and raisins. The batter will be loose. Do not worry if a few floury spots remain.

6 Fill each cavity of the prepared muffin tin almost to the top with the batter. Bake until a knife inserted in the center of a muffin comes out clean, 20 to 25 minutes. Turn out the baked muffins to cool on a rack. Serve warm.

VARIATIONS

Use shredded carrots and dark raisins in place of the zucchini and golden raisins. Or use a cup of well-squeezed, chopped cooked spinach together with the raisins and walnuts; for this version, add a few gratings of fresh nutmeg along with the cinnamon.

Blueberry Buttermilk Scones

YIELD: 4 SCONES

Making rich-tasting, flaky scones containing no cholesterol and only a modest amount of fat is no small feat. This recipe succeeds, producing light, fruit-studded scones that also offer a soy benefit.

1½ cups unbleached all-purpose flour
2 tablespoons soy flour
¼ cup unbleached cane sugar
1¼ teaspoons baking powder
¼ teaspoon double-acting baking soda
½ teaspoon orange zest
¼ teaspoon salt
⅓ cup Spectrum Spread, margarine, or unsalted butter
⅓ cup dried blueberries
6 tablespoons buttermilk

1 Preheat the oven to 375 degrees. Grease a baking sheet. Use a light-colored pan, since black bakeware makes the bottom of these scones color too easily.

2 In a bowl, whisk together the flour, soy flour, sugar, baking powder, baking soda, orange zest, and salt until well combined.

3 Using a fork, cut in the Spectrum Spread until the mixture is crumbly, with pea-size pieces. Mix in the blueberries.

4 Gradually add the buttermilk, mixing the dough with the fork or working it lightly with your fingertips until it just clings together but still looks slightly lumpy. You might not use all the buttermilk. Do not overwork the dough.

5 Dump the dough into the center of the prepared baking sheet. Pat it into an 8-inch disk. With a sharp knife, make 2 cuts almost through the dough in opposite directions, making a cross. This divides the dough into 4 scones.

6 Bake until the scones are golden. Take care they do not burn on the bottom. As soon as they are done in the center, after about 20 minutes, remove the scones from the baking sheet and let cool on a rack 20 minutes. Serve warm.

VARIATION

Use any dried fruit you like, perhaps cherries, cranberries, or raisins in place of the blueberries.

Apricot Butter

YIELD: 3 CUPS

Here is the essence of apricot flavor in a fat-free spread. It's heaven on a peanut butter sandwich or with cream cheese on a bagel. You can even eat it like applesauce, though the flavor is so intense that a little goes a long way. The absolutely best apricots for this recipe are dried Blenheims, a rare variety available only from the grower in California by mail (see page 229). Otherwise, use Turkish apricots, which are usually sweeter than those from California.

2 cups dried apricots
½ cup defrosted frozen apple juice concentrate
¼ cup unbleached cane sugar
1 to 2 teaspoons fresh lemon juice
½ package (5¼ ounces) soft or firm silken tofu

1 In a medium saucepan, combine the apricots, apple juice concentrate, cane sugar, lemon juice, and ¾ cup water. Bring to a boil, cover, reduce the heat, and simmer until the apricots are very soft, about 30 minutes (this varies, depending on how moist the apricots are).

2 With a slotted spoon, transfer the apricots to a blender. Add the cooking liquid. Process the apricots together with their liquid, until smooth. Add the tofu and process, stopping to scrape down the sides of the blender 2 to 3 times. Blend in the lemon juice. Transfer the apricot butter to a jar or plastic container. When it has cooled, cover tightly and refrigerate. This spread keeps 1 to 2 weeks in the refrigerator.

VARIATIONS

Add a Tahitian vanilla bean to the pot with the apricots and apple juice instead of vanilla extract. Take it out when the fruit is cooked. Using the bean adds so much natural sweetness that I halve the amount of sugar when making this variation.

If you see Himalayan dried apricots at a natural foods store, try them in this recipe. The result will look almost like apple butter and have astonishing, natural sweetness.

Samba Java Smoothie

YIELD: ONE 12-OUNCE DRINK

Here it is—fresh fruit, protein, coffee—everything you want
for breakfast, ready in minutes. This liquid meal provides
enough energy and flavor to make you samba through the
morning with a smile.

4 ice cubes
¼ cup soy powder
1 ripe banana, cut in 1-inch slices
1 shot of espresso, or ¼ cup strongly brewed fresh coffee,
    or 2 teaspoons instant coffee
¼ teaspoon ground cinnamon

Place the ice cubes, soy powder, banana, coffee, and cinnamon in a blender. Add 1 cup cold water. Process until the
cubes are crushed and the drink is creamy. Immediately pour
into a tall glass and serve.

VARIATION

If you like chocolate more than coffee, use unsweetened cocoa powder or extra-strength hot
cocoa in place of the java.

Strawberry Mint Smoothie

YIELD: ONE 12-OUNCE DRINK

On a warm day, you won't find a more refreshing and sustaining breakfast than this. The vanilla adds sweetness and the mint provides a stimulating lift.

1 cup frozen strawberries, unsweetened
¼ cup soy powder
¼ fresh mint leaves
1 teaspoon pure vanilla extract
1 to 2 tablespoons unbleached cane sugar (optional)
4 ice cubes

1 Place the strawberries, soy powder, mint, and vanilla in a blender. Add the sugar, if using. Add the ice cubes. Pour in 1 cup cold water. Blend until the drink is smooth and thick. Serve immediately.

VARIATIONS

Replace the mint with 1 tablespoon orange juice concentrate. For a thicker, sweeter smoothie, add a banana.

Rich Hot Cocoa

YIELD: 2 CUPS

My best friend Debby's mother used to serve us real hot cocoa made with milk and Van Houten's cocoa. Part of the charm was pouring it from the special, individual chocolate pots that came from Rumpelmeyer's, a fancy New York City tearoom. The richness of this hot cocoa lingers in my mind—dark, satiny, and bittersweet. I recommend buying Dutch-processed cocoa because it has a smoother taste and deeper flavor. And, of course, use a good-quality cocoa powder, such as Van Houten or Droste.

¼ cup unsweetened cocoa (Dutch-processed)
3 tablespoons unbleached cane sugar
1 tablespoon instant coffee
Pinch of salt
2 cups plain or vanilla regular soymilk
¼ teaspoon pure vanilla extract
Ground cinnamon (optional)

1 In a small saucepan, mix together the cocoa, sugar, coffee, and salt. Add ¼ cup of the soymilk and stir to make a paste.
2 Gradually pour in the remaining soy milk, stirring until the mixture is well blended.
3 Place the pot over medium heat and bring the cocoa almost to a boil, stirring occasionally. Take care not to let the cocoa boil.
4 Take the pot off the heat and stir in the vanilla. Pour the cocoa into mugs. Top with a dash of cinnamon, if desired.

Yogi Tea

YIELD: 4 SERVINGS

Recently, *chai*—black tea brewed with spices—has been growing in popularity as a stimulating alternative to coffee. This aromatic Indian beverage adds the digestive and soothing benefits of spices to the kick of caffeine.

3 pods cardamom, cracked
1 (3-inch) stick Ceylon cinnamon
2 whole cloves
½ teaspoon whole coriander
½ teaspoon fennel seeds
1 teaspoon black peppercorns
2 (2-inch) strips orange zest
1 tablespoon black tea (see note)
1 cup plain regular soymilk
2 tablespoons honey

1 In a medium saucepan, combine the cardamom, cinnamon, cloves, coriander, fennel, and peppercorns with the orange zest. Add 2 cups water and bring to a boil. Reduce the heat, cover, and simmer 5 minutes. Add the black tea. Cover and remove from the heat. Let steep 30 minutes.

2 Strain the spiced infusion. Pour it back into the pot. Add the soymilk and honey. Heat, pour into cups, and serve.

NOTE

If you avoid caffeine, use 5 decaffeinated tea bags.

Mail Order Sources

Over the years, I have found certain ingredients that are exceptional and companies that are reliable for shipping difficult to obtain ingredients. These are the choices I recommend.

Chile Peppers

Casados Farms, P.O. Box 852, San Juan Pueblo, NM 87566; (505) 852-2433.

Ships a selection of dried chile peppers.

Dried Fruit

American Spoon Foods, 1668 Clarion Ave., P.O. Box 566, Petoskey, MI 49770; (800) 222-5886 or (616) 347-9030.

Offers a wide variety of dried fruits.

Chukar Cherry Company, 320 Wine Country Road, P.O. Box 510, Prosser, WA 99530; (800) 624-9544.

Specializes in dried sweet and sour cherries.

Timber Crest Farms, 4791 Dry Creek Road, Healdsburg, CA 95448; (707) 433-8251.

A source for unsulfured dried fruit.

Gibson Farms, 1190 Buena Vista Road, Hollister, CA 95023; (408) 637-4183.

The only source for superb Blenheim dried apricots. Buy the "slabs."

Fresh Produce

Diamond Organics, Freedom, CA 95019; (800) 922-2396.

Ships a wide variety of beautiful, fresh, organic produce overnight. Surprisingly reasonable.

GRAINS AND DRIED BEANS

Bean Bag, 818 Jefferson St., Oakland, CA 94607; (800) 845-BEAN (845-2326).

Carries a wide assortment of dried beans.

Arrowhead Mills, P.O. Box 2059, Hereford, TX 79045; (800) 749-0730.

Sells grains, beans, and other natural and organic items by mail.

McSmith's Farm Produce, R.R. #6, St. Thomas, Ontario N5P 3T1; (519) 631-0279.

Grows Black Jet soybeans. Sells them dried, in 1-pound bags.

HERBS AND SPICES

Penzey's Spice House Ltd., P.O. Box 1448, Waukesha, WI 53187; (414) 574-0277; fax (414) 574-0278.

Carries freshly ground spices and dried herbs and seasonings. Their pure vanilla extract is outstanding.

Fox Hill Farm, 444 West Michigan Ave., Box 79, Parma, MI 49269; (517) 531-3179.

Grows and ships fresh herbs.

Frontier Cooperative Herbs, Box 299, Norway, IA 52318; (800) 669-3275.

Offers a wide range of organic dried herbs, and spices that are not irradiated or fumigated.

MAPLE SYRUP

Uncle Joel's Pure Maple Syrup, 1988 County Road YY, Baldwin, WI 54002; (715) 684-4787.

MISO

South River Miso Co., Inc., South River Farm, Conway, MA 01341; (413) 369-4057; fax (413) 369-4299.

Makes and sells artisanally produced miso and miso tamari.

Mushrooms

Aux Delices Des Bois, 4 Leonard St., New York, NY 10013; (800) 666-1232 or (212) 334-1230.

Ships a wide variety of fresh and dried mushrooms.

Natural Foods

Gold Mine Natural Food Co., 3419 Hancock St., San Diego, CA 92110; (800) 475-3663.

Carries a wide variety of natural foods, including miso.

Textured Vegetable Protein (TVP)

The Mail Order Catalog, P.O. Box 180-TC, Summertown, TN 38483; (800) 695-2241.

This is the best-tasting TVP, available in a variety of sizes, plain or with flavorings.

Wild Rice

Black Duck Company, 10932 Glen Wilding Place, Bloomington, MN 55431; (612) 884-3472.

A reasonably priced source for wild rice.

Bibliography

Bloodroot Collective, The. *The Second Seasonal Cookbook*. Bridgeport, CT: Sanguinaria Publishing, 1984.

Elliot, Rose. *The Complete Vegetarian Cuisine*. New York: Pantheon Books, 1988.

Lanza, Anna Tasca. *The Heart of Sicily*. New York: Clarkson Potter, 1993.

Marks, Copeland. *The Korean Table*. Chronicle Books, 1993.

McDermott, Nanci. *Real Thai*. Chronicle Books, 1992.

Messina, Mark, and Virginia Messina. *The Simple Soybean and Your Health*. Garden City Park, NY: Avery Publishing Group, 1994.

Millon, Marc, and Kim Millon. *Flavours of Korea*. London: Andre Deutsch, 1994.

Mindell, Earl. *Earl Mindell's Soy Miracle*. New York: Simon & Schuster, 1995.

Netzer, Corinne T. *The Complete Book of Food Counts*. New York: Dell, 1994.

Sax, Richard. *Classic Home Desserts*. Shelburne, VT: Chapters, 1994.

Shurtleff, William, and Akiko Aoyagi. *The Book of Miso*. Berkeley, CA: Ten Speed Press, 1976.

———. *The Book of Tempeh*. New York: Harper & Row, 1979.

———. *The Book of Tofu*. New York: Ballantine, 1979.

Tsuji, Shizuo. *Japanese Cooking—A Simple Art*. Kodansha International, 1980.

Waldron, Maggie. *Cold Spaghetti at Midnight*. William Morrow & Co., 1992.

Wittenberg, Margaret M. *Good Food: The Complete Guide to Eating Well*. Freedom, CA: The Crossing Press, 1995.

INDEX

Index
••••

Cotton tofu, 5
Cranberries
  Apple Cranberry Crumble, 192–193
  Breakfast Rice Pudding, 216–217
Cream cheese, tofu, 39
  Creamy Basil Cheesecake, 114–116
  Spinach Baklava, 129–131
The Creamiest Tofu Cheesecake in the
    World, 194–196
Creamy Basil Cheesecake, 114–116
Creamy Dessert Topping, 204
Creamy Miso Gravy, 150–151
Creamy Ranch Dressing, 168–169
Croutons, Garlic Tempeh, 170–171
Cucumbers, Greek Salad with "Feta,"
    160–161
Cumin, 39
Currants
  Breakfast Rice Pudding, 216–217
  Mincemeat Croustade, 197–199
  Stuffed French Toast, 212–213
Curries
  Indonesian Coconut Apple Curry, 98–99
  Red Curried Tofu, 100–101

D

Dairy-Free Pie Crust, 184–185
Dairy products, soy, 23–24
Dandelion-leek miso, 14
Danko, Gary, 106–109
Dashi, Udon with Miso-Glazed Eggplant,
    132–133
Dean Foods, 27
Defatting process, 23
Defrosting tofu, 32–33
Deli foods, soy, 24–25
Desserts. See also Cheesecakes; Pies;
    Puddings; Toppings
  Apple Cranberry Crumble, 192–193
  Banana Coconut Bread Pudding,
      188–189
  Chocolate Silk Pie, 182–183
  The Creamiest Tofu Cheesecake in the
      World, 194–196
  Double Chocolate Pudding, 190–191
  Gingerbread, 202–204
  Indian Pudding, 200–201
  Italian Cheese Pie, 185, 186–187
  Mincemeat Croustade, 197–199
Dijon Mustard Tofu Cream, 165–166
Dill, Egyptian Parsley Salad, 162–163
Dips
  Aioli, 66–67

Sun-Dried Tomato Dip, 64–65
Double Chocolate Pudding, 190–191
Dressings
  Creamy Ranch Dressing, 168–169
  Pepper Ranch Dressing, 169
  Real Russian Dressing, 167
Dried black soybeans. See Black soybeans
Dried chili powder, 125
Dried fruit, mail order sources for, 229
Droste cocoa, 226
Dry rubs on tofu, 33

E

Edamame, 26–27
Eden Foods, 15
EdenSoy, 38
Eggless Egg Salad, 165–166
Eggplant
  Tofu "Scallops" Ritz Carlton, 206–209
  Udon with Miso-Glazed Eggplant,
      132–133
Eggs, Greek Salad with "Feta," 160–161
Egyptian Parsley Salad, 162–163
Elwell, Christian and Margaret, ix, 10
Enzymes
  in miso, 14–15
  in tempeh, 18
Epsom salts, 5
Extra-firm tofu, 7

F

Fakin' Bacon, 121
The Farm, Summertown, Tennessee, 18
  protein, 26
  textured vegetable protein (TVP), 26
Farmer's markets, 41–42
Farm Vegetarian Cookbook, 18
Fat content
  of soymilk, 20, 38
  of tofu, 8–9
Fermented bean paste. See Miso
"Feta," Greek Salad with, 160–161
Firm tofu, 7
Flan, Carrot with Pistachios, 122–123
Flavorings, 39–40
Florida Crystals, 43
Frankfurters, soy, 25
Franklin, Benjamin, 4
Freezing tofu, 32–33
French Toast, Stuffed, 212–213
Fresh produce, mail order sources, 229
Fresh soybeans, 26–27
Fresh tofu, 31

Index
••••

Index
• • • •